Lecture Notes in Bioinformatics 12686

Subseries of Lecture Notes in Computer Science

More information about this subseries at http://www.springer.com/series/5381

Sumit Kumar Jha · Ion Măndoiu ·
Sanguthevar Rajasekaran · Pavel Skums ·
Alex Zelikovsky (Eds.)

Computational Advances in Bio and Medical Sciences

10th International Conference, ICCABS 2020
Virtual Event, December 10–12, 2020
Revised Selected Papers

 Springer

Editors
Sumit Kumar Jha ⓘ
The University of Texas at San Antonio
San Antonio, TX, USA

Sanguthevar Rajasekaran ⓘ
University of Connecticut
Storrs Mansfield, CT, USA

Alex Zelikovsky ⓘ
Department of Computer Science
Georgia State University
Atlanta, GA, USA

Ion Măndoiu ⓘ
University of Connecticut
Storrs, CT, USA

Pavel Skums ⓘ
Department of Computer Science
Georgia State University
Roswell, GA, USA

ISSN 0302-9743   ISSN 1611-3349 (electronic)
Lecture Notes in Bioinformatics
ISBN 978-3-030-79289-3   ISBN 978-3-030-79290-9   (eBook)
https://doi.org/10.1007/978-3-030-79290-9

LNCS Sublibrary: SL8 – Bioinformatics

This Springer imprint is published by the registered company Springer Nature Switzerland AG
The registered company address is: Gewerbestrasse 11, 6330 Cham, Switzerland

Preface

The 10th edition of the International Conference on Computational Advances in Bio and medical Sciences (ICCABS 2020) was held in a virtual format during December 10–12, 2020. ICCABS has the goal of bringing together researchers, scientists, and students from academia, laboratories, and industry to discuss recent advances on computational techniques and applications in the areas of biology, medicine, and drug discovery.

There were 11 extended abstracts submitted in response to the ICCABS 2020 call for papers. Following a rigorous review process in which each submission was reviewed by at least two Program Committee members, the Program Committee decided to accept six extended abstracts for oral presentation and publication in the post-proceedings volume. The technical program of ICCABS 2020 included 15 invited talks presented at the 10th Workshop on Computational Advances for Next Generation Sequencing (CANGS 2020) and 15 invited talks presented at the 3rd Workshop on Computational Advances for Single-Cell Omics Data Analysis (CASCODA 2020). Workshop speakers were invited to submit extended abstracts and, following the same review process used for the main conference, five additional extended abstracts were selected for publication in the post-proceedings volume. All extended abstracts included in the volume have been revised to address reviewers' comments.

The technical program of ICCABS 2020 also featured keynote talks by three distinguished speakers: Prof. Leslie M. Loew from the University of Connecticut Health Center, USA, gave a talk on "The Virtual Cell Project," Prof. May Dongmei Wang from the Georgia Institute of Technology and Emory University, USA, gave a talk on "Translating AI for Biomedicine and Healthcare: Challenges and Opportunities," and Prof. Amarda Shehu from George Mason University, USA, gave a talk on "Great Disruptions and Expectations: A Perspective in Protein Modeling Research." We would like to thank all keynote speakers and authors for presenting their work at the conference. We would also like to thank the Program Committee members and external reviewers for volunteering their time to review and discuss the submissions. Last but not least, we would like to extend special thanks to the Steering Committee members for their continued leadership, and to the finance, local arrangements, publicity, and publication chairs for their hard work in making ICCABS 2020 a successful event despite the ongoing COVID-19 pandemic.

May 2021

Sumit Kumar Jha
Ion Măndoiu
Sanguthevar Rajasekaran
Pavel Skums
Alex Zelikovsky

Organization

Steering Committee

Srinivas Aluru	Georgia Institute of Technology, USA
Reda A. Ammar	University of Connecticut, USA
Tao Jiang	University of California, Riverside, USA
Vipin Kumar	University of Minnesota, USA
Ming Li	University of Waterloo, Canada
Sanguthevar Rajasekaran (Chair)	University of Connecticut, USA
John Reif	Duke University, USA
Sartaj Sahni	University of Florida, USA

General Chairs

Sanguthevar Rajasekaran	University of Connecticut, USA
Sartaj Sahni	University of Florida, USA

Program Chair

Sumit Kumar Jha	University of Central Florida, USA

Workshop Chairs

Ion Măndoiu	University of Connecticut, USA
Pavel Skums	Georgia State University, USA
Alex Zelikovsky	Georgia State University, USA

Finance Chair

Reda A. Ammar	University of Connecticut, USA

Local Arrangements Chairs

Ahmed Soliman	University of Connecticut, USA
Haarith Vohra	University of Connecticut, USA
Yijue Wang	University of Connecticut, USA

Publication Chair

Zigeng Wang	University of Connecticut, USA

Publicity Chairs

Orlando Echevarria   University of Connecticut, USA
Bob Weiner   University of Connecticut, USA

Webmaster

Zigeng Wang   University of Connecticut, USA

Program Committee

Max Alekseyev   George Washington University, USA
Dwaipayan Chakraborty   Rowan University, USA
Jaime Davila   Mayo Clinic, USA
Jorge Duitama   Universidad de los Andes, Columbia
Richard Edwards   University of New South Wales, Australia
Oliver Eulenstein   Iowa State University, USA
Steven Fernandes   Creighton University, USA
Sumit Kumar Jha   University of Texas at San Antonio, USA
Danny Krizanc   Wesleyan University, USA
M. Oguzhan Kulekci   Istanbul Technical University, Turkey
Manuel Lafond   Université de Sherbrooke, Canada
Yuk Yee Leung   University of Pennsylvania, USA
Maria Poptsova   HSE University, Russia
Sunny Raj   Oakland University, USA
Subrata Saha   IBM, USA
Pavel Skums   Georgia State University, USA
Sing-Hoi Sze   Texas A&M University, USA
Sharma V. Thankachan   University of Central Florida, USA
Ugo Vaccaro   University of Salerno, Italy
Balaji Venkatachalam   Google, USA
Jianxin Wang   Central South University, China
Fang Xiang Wu   University of Saskatchewan, Canada
Shibu Yooseph   University of Central Florida, USA
Shaojie Zhang   University of Central Florida, USA
Wei Zhang   University of Central Florida, USA
Cuncong Zhong   University of Kansas, USA

Additional Reviewers

Abedin, Paniz   Kuzmin, Kirill
Bansal, Mukul S.   Patterson, Murray
Duitama, Jorge   Saghaian, Hossein
Howard-Stone, Rye   Tavakoli, Neda
Icer, Pelin Burcak   Tsyvina, Viachaslau

Contents

Computational Advances in Bio and Medical Sciences

DNA Read Feature Importance Using Machine Learning for Read Alignment Categories

Jacob S. Porter[✉][ID]

Biocomplexity Institute and Initiative, University of Virginia,
Charlottesville, VA, USA
jsporter@virginia.edu

Abstract. An empirical understanding of how DNA read features affect read alignment quality categories is useful in designing better read mapping and alignment software, read trimmers, and sequence masks. Many programs appear to use arbitrarily chosen features that are putatively relevant to DNA alignment quality. Machine learning gives a ready way to empirically assess a variety of features and rank them according to their importance. Sequence complexity features such as run length distribution, DUST, and entropy, and quality measures from the DNA read data were used to predict read alignment quality categories on Ion Torrent and Illumina data sets using both bisulfite-treated and untreated short DNA reads. Run length mean and variance did as well or better than the DUST score and entropy, even though several programs use the DUST score and entropy. Sequence compression features performed poorly. Predictive accuracy of the models had F1-scores between 0.5–0.95 indicating that the feature set can fairly well predict alignment categories.

Keywords: DNA alignment · Machine learning · Sequence complexity

1 Introduction

A DNA read sequencer produces DNA fragments called reads. A DNA read is a string over the alphabet $\{A, C, T, G, N\}$ corresponding to the nucleotide bases and the N wildcard character. DNA sequence alignment programs map these DNA reads to a reference genome. This process can be error prone as the DNA fragments may not match a portion of the reference genome perfectly because of natural variation and mutation or because of sequencing error [24,30].

DNA sequence mapping software that is used for regular untreated reads includes Bowtie2 [9], BWA [11], and BFAST [6]. Mapping software for bisulfite-treated reads must adjust for the bisulfite treatment, and such software includes Bismark [8], BWA-Meth [17], and BisPin [22]. Bisulfite treatment is used to search for covalent modification of cytosine in DNA. There are many more examples of alignment and mapping software.

© Springer Nature Switzerland AG 2021
S. K. Jha et al. (Eds.): ICCABS 2020, LNBI 12686, pp. 3–14, 2021.
https://doi.org/10.1007/978-3-030-79290-9_1

Insight into which read features are important to alignment quality categories could lead to more effective alignment software, read trimmers, masking algorithms, and so on. I used machine learning to study which numerical features of short DNA reads are predictive of read alignment quality categories. These features include metrics of quality, sequence complexity, and sequence compressibility.

2   Related Work and Motivation

I used machine learning to predict up to four read alignment categories as discussed in Sect. 3.2. Four classifiers were trained for each data set for each mapping software.

My purpose wasn't to use machine learning to predict alignment categories since learning the categories can be done simply by running the alignment software. My purpose was to explore features relevant to read alignment quality. However, simple machine learning approaches could be used to efficiently filter out predicted low quality reads, and so forth. This is explored in Sect. 4.4.

Assessing feature relevance allows for good decisions to be made in their use in bioinformatics software. Trimming and masking software such as InfoTrim and Cookiecutter use sequence complexity [21,28]. The bisulfite software Bat-Meth has a low complexity filter using Shannon entropy [14], and BLAST uses the DUST score for complexity masking [1,15]. The DUST score measures trinucleotide frequency. The sequence complexity measures chosen for these programs appear to be arbitrarily chosen or chosen for convenience. Compression software has been used to determine sequence similarity [31]. A thorough evaluation of such measures with machine learning gives an empirical rationale for the choice of the sequence complexity measures.

Other work has used machine learning to predict DNA function from DNA sequence identity [13] and methylation loci from DNA reads [32]. My own study found that Shannon entropy corresponds to read alignment categories [20]. A study found that genome complexity relates to read mapping quality [19], but my study examines reads rather than genomes.

3   Methods

Reads were mapped using typical alignment programs, and standard machine learning approaches were used to predict alignment categories. Custom Python program were used for feature extraction.

3.1   Data Acquisition and Read Mapping

Six data sets of three million reads each were downloaded from the sequence read archive (SRA) [10] at https://www.ncbi.nlm.nih.gov/sra. This data represents a variety of bisulfite-treated and regular short DNA reads. Bisuflite- treated reads are used to search for epigenetic cytosine covalent modifications, and these reads were included since aligning these reads can be challenging with low alignment quality [20, 29]. The data includes quality information that gives the probability that the base was called correctly. No trimming was performed.

The data includes DNA reads generated from the Illumina platform and the Ion Torrent platform. Ion Torrent sequencers create variable length reads from 100–300 base pairs with greater error in homopolymer runs [23]. Illumina technology creates reads of uniform length that can be a bit shorter than Ion Torrent reads. Illumina technology is much more common, and it can generate 'paired-end' reads. Table 1 shows a summary of the data used. This data set represents a variety of sequencing technologies and platforms, so it useful for generalizing the results.

Table 1. Summary of the DNA read data.

SRA #	Type	Platform	Len	Species	Mappers
ERR2562409	BS	Illumina	90	Mouse	BisPin, Bismark
SRR1104850	BS	Illumina	200	Human	BisPin
SRR5144899	BS	Illumina	101	Human	BisPin, Bismark
SRR1534392	BS	Ion Torrent	Varies	Mouse	BisPin, Tabsat
SRR2172246	Reg	Illumina	76	Human	BFAST, Bowtie2
ERR699568	Reg	Ion Torrent	Varies	Mouse	BFAST-Gap, TMAP

One or two read mapping and alignment programs were used to map and align each data set to the reference genome. The GRCh38.p9 human reference genome was used, and the GRCm38.p5 mouse reference genome was used. These genomes can be downloaded from the NCBI (National Center for Biotechnology Information) data store at https://www.ncbi.nlm.nih.gov/genome. Table 1 indicates which read mapping programs were used with which data set. Thus, eleven alignment files were created to do machine learning.

For bisulfite-treated Illumina reads, BisPin [22] and Bismark [8] were used on their default settings. A primary and secondary index was used with BisPin with rescoring turned off. Bismark is a popular read mapper for bisulfite-treated reads, and it uses Bowtie2 [9] to do alignments. BisPin is a versatile read mapper that has good accuracy with a variety of data [22]. Bismark did not return any mapped reads for data set SRR1104850, so only BisPin was used there. For Illumina regular untreated reads, BFAST (BLAT-like Fast Accurate Search Tool) [6] and Bowtie2 [9] were used.

For bisulfite-treated Ion Torrent reads, BisPin and Tabsat were used. BisPin was used with default settings appropriate to Ion Torrent reads as found in [22]. Tabsat [16] uses Bismark's Perl code and the Ion Torrent read mapper TMAP (Torrent Mapping Alignment Program https://github.com/iontorrent/TMAP). For regular untreated Ion Torrent reads, BFAST-Gap [22] and TMAP were used. TMAP was used with the map4 algorithm.

3.2   Feature and Class Extraction

Feature Extraction. For each DNA read, 67 numerical features were created that comprised sequence complexity, read content, compressibility, and quality. Reads with N's in them were excluded from the analysis as their presence interferes with the sequence complexity measures; however, N's are highly relevant to read mapper performance as an N means an ambiguous nucleotide base that can match to any nucleotide base in the reference genome.

The sequence complexity features included run length metrics, the DUST score, entropy, $D_k(a)$, $R_k(a)$, Bzip2 compressibility, and LZMA compressibility. Compressibility is related to sequence complexity [12], and it has been used to measure DNA sequence similarity [31].

The run length distribution was computed. A run is a substring of the DNA string comprised of the same base. The length of the run is the number of bases in that run. For example, "AATCCC" has a length 2 run of A's, a length 1 run of a T, and a length 3 run of C's. The mean, variance, and maximum of this distribution were used as features.

The DUST score is a sequence complexity metric based on tri-nucleotide frequency [15]. A search of the literature did not reveal why this metric is called DUST. Given that a is a sequence of n characters from $\mathcal{A} = \{A, C, T, G\}$, a *triplet* is a substring of length 3, and there are 64 possible triplets. The space of triplets is $\mathcal{R}$. There are $n - 2$ non-unique triplets in a for $n > 2$. If $c_t(a)$ is the number of times triplet t occurs in a, then the DUST score is

$$\frac{\sum_{t \in \mathcal{R}} c_t(a)(c_t(a) - 1)/2}{n - 3}.$$

The DUST score was normalized to be between 0 and 1 by dividing it by $\frac{(n-2)(n-3)/2}{n-3}$, the maximum DUST score.

Shannon entropy [26] is a sequence complexity measure common in machine learning. If $f_b(a)$ is the frequency of character b in sequence a, then entropy is given by

$$-\sum_{b \in \mathcal{A}} f_b(a) \log_2(f_b(a)).$$

For each $b \in \mathcal{A}$, the base frequency $f_b(a)$ was included as a feature. This captures sequence content related features.

The metrics $D_k(a)$ and $R_k(a)$ are found in [19]. The function $g(x)$ gives the number of times that the substring x occurs in a. $D_k(a)$ measures the rate of distinct substrings. Given a number k for the substring length, $D_k(a)$ is defined as

$$D_k(a) = \frac{|\{x : g(x) > 0 \,|\, |x| = k, x \in a\}|}{|a| - k + 1}.$$

$R_k(a)$ measures the rate of repeats, and it is

$$R_k(a) = \frac{\sum_{g(x) > 1, |x| = k} g(x)}{|a| - k + 1}.$$

$R_k(a)$ and $D_k(a)$ for $k = 2, 3, 4, 5$ were used. These metrics can be computed in linear time and space using suffix arrays [19].

The Bzip2 and LZMA implementations in Python3 were used to measure the compressibility of the DNA sequence. The number of bytes returned by the compression algorithms was divided by the length of the uncompressed sequence to get a compressibility metric.

Quality related features were computed from the probability measures given with the DNA reads. This included the mean, variance, skewness, maximum, and minimum. Since the probabilities are arranged in a sequence, the difference between each probability was computed, and these values were averaged and included as a feature.

The preceding features were computed for the whole read. For each third of the DNA sequence, each of the preceding features except for $D_k(a)$, $R_k(a)$ and the run length metrics, were computed and included in the feature set as well.

Label Extraction. This problem was modeled as a classification problem since every read mapping program gives some indication of read alignment uniqueness. For each read in an alignment file, the FLAG field of the SAM alignment record was inspected to assign the read into one of four classes: uniquely mapped, ambiguously mapped, unmapped, and filtered.

A read is uniquely mapped if the read mapping software reports that there is a unique best scoring alignment for that read. A read is ambiguously mapped if there are multiple best scoring locations. An unmapped read maps to no location, and a filtered read has an alignment score below some program specific threshold. Not every read mapper reports every class, so some classes were excluded for some read mappers. One of these classes is predicted for each read.

3.3   Machine Learning Methods

Python3 with scikit-learn 0.19.1 [18] was used to do machine learning. Four machine learning classifiers were used to assess predictive accuracy: random assignment (Rand), random forest (RF), multi-layer perceptron neural network (MLP), and logistic regression (LR). All features were centered and scaled using the StandardScaler in scikit-learn for each classifier for each data set. Because there were eleven alignment results, eleven machine learning models were created for each classifier type and for each software for a total of 44 trained classifiers.

A random classifier (Rand) was trained. This classifier learns the proportion of classes in the training data and simply guesses a class with probability equal to the proportion that it learned for that class. This classifier was used to determine if the other three classifiers were better than random guessing.

A random forest is an ensemble of decision trees. At each level in the tree, a value for a feature is used to split the level. The leaves are labeled with classes. An MLP is a neural network with hidden layers that linearly combine previous layers and apply an activation function. The ReLU activation function was used. The output of the network is a vector of probabilities for each class. Logistic regression is a binary statistical model that uses a log-odds ratio. It was used with the l2 norm. A binary problem was used for each class, and the class with the maximum probability was reported as the predicted class [5].

Bayesian optimization with scikit-optimize was used to do hyperparameter tuning with three-fold cross-validation. Bayesian optimization strategically selects a point in the hyper-parameter space based on the performance of previously selected hyperparameters [27]. The GP-hedge acquisition function was used, and twenty-five iterations were performed.

Random forest hyperparameters max depth and max features were optimized. After some experiments, a MLP architecture with four hidden layers of size 30, 20, 15, and 10 was chosen, and the regularization parameter alpha was optimized. Logistic regression uses a regularization parameter that was optimized.

Three-fold cross validation was used to train on 2.5 million training examples. Approximately 500,000 reads were held-out as test data to assess model predictive performance. Reads with N's were excluded from the analysis. Cohen's kappa metric was used for model selection since it is supposed to perform better than accuracy with rare classes [3]. Precision, recall, and the F1-score (the harmonic mean of precision and recall) were computed for each class for each data set. These were used to assess predictive performance on the held-out test data.

The source code and a results spreadsheet can be found at:
https://github.com/JacobPorter/AlignmentML.

4   Results

Models' F1-scores ranged from 0.5–0.95. The most important features were sequence complexity features. Quality and compression features were less important. A read filter based on trained machine learning models found improvements in some data.

4.1   Model Accuracy

The F1-score was computed for each class, and then each class's F1-score was averaged to assess model predictive performance. These results are presented in Table 2. The mapping classes are represented as letters (U = Unique, A = Ambig, N = Unmapped, F = Filtered). All models performed better than random guessing. Random forest models always had the highest F1-score, and logistic regression was generally the worst with the slowest training time. The MLP had the fastest training time of the three.

Predictive accuracy was generally good for uniquely mapped reads and poor for ambiguously mapped reads. Predictive accuracy for unmapped and filtered reads ranged from poor to fair. The number of uniquely mapped reads could be as high as approximately 90% of the data, and other classes could only be a few percent of the data. This makes non-unique classes rare and prediction difficult.

Table 2. Average class F1-score for each data set.

Data	Software	Classes	Rand	RF	MLP	LR
ERR2562409	Bismark	UAN	0.40	0.94	0.84	0.80
ERR2562409	BisPin	UANF	0.41	0.95	0.85	0.81
ERR699568	BFAST-Gap	UANF	0.86	0.91	0.90	0.90
ERR699568	TMAP	UA	0.87	0.92	0.91	0.91
SRR1104850	BisPin	UANF	0.52	0.77	0.77	0.74
SRR1534392	BisPin	UANF	0.59	0.82	0.73	0.72
SRR1534392	Tabsat	UAN	0.68	0.88	0.84	0.80
SRR2172246	BFAST	UANF	0.34	0.53	0.51	0.49
SRR2172246	Bowite2	UA	0.84	0.92	0.90	0.90
SRR5144899	Bismark	UAN	0.65	0.81	0.80	0.79
SRR5144899	BisPin	UANF	0.72	0.85	0.82	0.81

An example of precision, recall, and F1-score by class is shown in Table 3. The 'Read amount' column gives the number of reads in the class. Throughout this project, precision was generally better than recall, and Ambig was the class that was generally the hardest to predict. This may be because the ambiguously mapped class may have sequence complexity intermediate between uniquely mapped and unmapped reads [20] making the difference more difficult to distinguish. Ambiguously mapped reads may be a result of repetition in the genome [4,25] that can't be detected from examining the read alone.

Table 3. Precision, recall, and F1-Score by class for SRR5144899 Bismark.

Class	Precision	Recall	F1-Score	Read amount
Unique	0.851	0.974	0.909	393343
Ambig	0.657	0.133	0.221	36771
Unmap	0.775	0.473	0.587	69094

4.2   Feature Importance

Random forest feature importance was used to rank the features since the random forest models had the best predictive performance. This gives a ranking of features from most important to least important according to the model. This ranking was computed for each of the eleven data sets, and the distribution of ranks for each feature was computed. Figure 1 gives a notched box plot of these distributions for all of the features that used the entire read. Qual features are quality features. LZMA and bz2 are compression features, and all other features are related to sequence complexity.

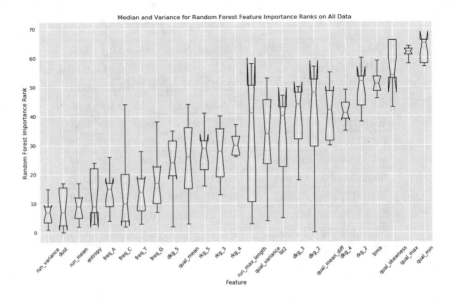

Fig. 1. Feature importances for all of the data. For each data set and each read mapper, random forest feature rank importances were calculated, and the distribution of rank for each feature was used to make the box plot. $D_k(a)$ is referred to as dkg, and $R_k(a)$ is referred to as rkg.

Run length variance and run length mean were among the most important and performed a bit better than entropy and the DUST score in some cases. This is interesting since several programs use the DUST score, such as BLAST [1,15], and entropy [14,21]. Run length metrics could be as good or better if they replaced the DUST score and entropy. Character frequency features were of good importance but not as important as the DUST score and entropy.

$D_k(a)$ and $R_k(a)$ performed more poorly; however, $D_2(a)$ was very important for the data ERR2562409 as it was ranked the most important with an average importance confidence 0.251, which was larger by 0.174 on average than the next best feature, the largest difference of its kind. Perhaps $D_k(a)$ is more useful for some data sets.

Compressibility measures were the worst average performing sequence complexity metrics. LZMA was the worst on average with a mean rank of 51.45. However, the Bzip2 feature from the first third of the sequence had the highest rank on the SRR1534392 data with BisPin, and LZMA in the second third of the sequence had the highest rank for the SRR1534392 data with Tabsat.

Quality metrics were generally not as important as sequence complexity metrics. The quality mean was the most important of these, and quality skewness, maximum, and minimum had the lowest importance of all features.

Since four of the six data sets were for bisulfite-sequencing reads, there could be a bias favoring bisulfite read mapping. Thus, the same feature rank analysis was performed with only the regular untreated data. The feature rank notched box plots for this data can be found in Fig. 2. The order of features is very similar, but the DUST score does a little better, outperforming the run length metrics. The quality mean is a bit lower in the rankings.

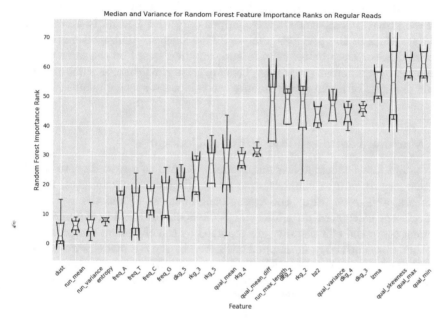

Fig. 2. Feature importances for the regular untreated data. $D_k(a)$ is referred to as dkg, and $R_k(a)$ is referred to as rkg.

In Illumina data sets, features from the last third of the read generally had a higher importance than features in the first or second thirds of the read sequence. Features from the second third were generally more important than features from the first third. This may be because there is often lower quality in the last third of a read since Illumina sequencing technology can make more errors in later cycles [2]. In Ion Torrent data, features from each third were generally more evenly distributed in the top 15 most important features.

4.3   Feature Ranking Similarity Across Different Data

There is weak evidence that the feature importance ranking depends more on the read mapper than the data set. This conclusion was drawn by looking at Kendall's tau coefficient for feature rankings across different data. Kendall's tau coefficient is used to measure how similar two ordered sequences are [7]. It ranges from 1.0 to −1.0. A 1.0 means the sequences are identical, and a −1.0 means that the sequences are the reverse of each other.

Kendall's tau coefficient and p-value were computed using scipy. The feature importance ranking for both read mappers for the same SRA number was used to calculate Kendall's tau. Only ERR2562409 and ERR699568 had p-values below 0.1. All tau's were positive. The highest was for ERR699568 at 0.308, and the lowest was for SRR5144899 at 0.0276. Both data sets come from bisulfite-treated Illumina reads.

The feature importance ranking for all data mapped with BisPin was compared with SRR1104850 since it was mapped only with BisPin. In all cases, tau was larger than in the previous analysis. This suggests that read mapper feature rankings correlate better than feature rankings based on the same data set but mapped by different programs. This suggests that there is some program-specific qualities of feature performance, and data set specific qualities are less important.

4.4   Machine Learning Filter Proof-of-Concept

The random forest machine learning model was used as a read filter to test the idea that these features could lead to more effective read trimmers, masking algorithms, and so on. First, the average alignment score and the average edit distance were calculated on additional 300k–500k reads after alignment. The alignment score and edit distance are reported by the alignment program. Then, reads that were marked as unmapped or filtered by the RF model were excluded, and the averages were calculated. Table 4 summarizes the results. A positive number represents an improvement while a negative number represents a loss. The 200bp data set SRR1104850 had slightly worse alignments on average, but the other data sets showed a bigger improvement. This validates that these methods can be used as a low complexity filter to improve alignments.

Table 4. Differences in alignment score and edit distance for filtered reads.

Data	Mapper	Alignment diff	Edit diff
SRR2172246	BFAST	626.47	5.06
SRR5144899	BisPin	2283.69	6.86
SRR1104850	BisPin	−110.59	−2.03

5   Conclusions

My study showed that sequence complexity measures are important in predicting the read mapping quality of short DNA reads. Read quality metrics were less important. Run length mean and variance, the DUST score, and entropy were the best performing sequence complexity measures. Bioinformatics programs may consider using run length statistics because they were among the best features.

Without knowledge of the genome, and only knowledge of the DNA read, machine learning models, especially random forests, were able to predict alignment quality with surprisingly good accuracy approaching F1-scores of 0.95. The features that work well on regular untreated reads tended to work well on bisulfite reads. This suggests that sequence complexity measures that work well in one application will probably work well in other applications.

Future work could include training a regressor to predict the alignment score rather than alignment categories; however not all programs (such as Bismark) report such a score. A model with very few features that predicts the alignment score could make a fast read filter. The effect of read trimming can be explored.

References

1. Altschul, S.F., Gish, W., Miller, W., Myers, E.W., Lipman, D.J.: Basic local alignment search tool. J. Mol. Biol. **215**(3), 403–410 (1990)
2. Buermans, H., Den Dunnen, J.: Next generation sequencing technology: advances and applications. Biochimica et Biophysica Acta (BBA)-Mol. Basis Dis. **1842**(10), 1932–1941 (2014)
3. Cohen, J.: A coefficient of agreement for nominal scales. Educ. Psychol. Meas. **20**(1), 37–46 (1960)
4. Deininger, P.: Alu elements: know the sines. Genome Biol. **12**(12), 236 (2011)
5. Friedman, J., Hastie, T., Tibshirani, R.: The Elements of Statistical Learning. SSS, vol. 12. Springer, New York (2001). https://doi.org/10.1007/978-0-387-21606-5
6. Homer, N., Merriman, B., Nelson, S.F.: BFAST: an alignment tool for large scale genome resequencing. PLOS One **4**(11), e7767 (2009)
7. Kendall, M.G.: A new measure of rank correlation. Biometrika **30**(1/2), 81–93 (1938)
8. Krueger, F., Andrews, S.R.: Bismark: a flexible aligner and methylation caller for Bisulfite-Seq applications. Bioinformatics **27**(11), 1571–1572 (2011)
9. Langmead, B., Salzberg, S.L.: Fast gapped-read alignment with Bowtie 2. Nat. Methods **9**(4), 357 (2012)
10. Leinonen, R., Sugawara, H., Shumway, M., International Nucleotide Sequence Database Collaboration: The sequence read archive. Nucleic Acids Res. **39**(1), D19–D21 (2010)
11. Li, H., Durbin, R.: Fast and accurate short read alignment with Burrows-Wheeler transform. Bioinformatics **25**(14), 1754–1760 (2009)
12. Li, M., Vitányi, P.: An Introduction to Kolmogorov Complexity and its Applications. TCS, Springer, New York (2008). https://doi.org/10.1007/978-0-387-49820-1
13. Libbrecht, M.W., Noble, W.S.: Machine learning applications in genetics and genomics. Nat. Rev. Genetics **16**(6), 321 (2015)
14. Lim, J.Q., et al.: BatMeth: improved mapper for bisulfite sequencing reads on DNA methylation. Genome Biol. **13**(10), R82 (2012)
15. Morgulis, A., Gertz, E.M., Schäffer, A.A., Agarwala, R.: A fast and symmetric DUST implementation to mask low-complexity DNA sequences. J. Comput. Biol. **13**(5), 1028–1040 (2006)
16. Pabinger, S., et al.: Analysis and visualization tool for targeted amplicon bisulfite sequencing on Ion Torrent sequencers. PloS One **11**(7), e0160227 (2016)
17. Pedersen, B.S., Eyring, K., De, S., Yang, I.V., Schwartz, D.A.: Fast and accurate alignment of long bisulfite-seq reads. arXiv preprint arXiv:1401.1129 (2014)
18. Pedregosa, F., et al.: Scikit-learn: machine learning in Python. J. Mach. Learn. Res. **12**, 2825–2830 (2011)

19. Phan, V., Gao, S., Tran, Q., Vo, N.S.: How genome complexity can explain the difficulty of aligning reads to genomes. BMC Bioinform. **16**(17), S3 (2015)
20. Porter, J., Sun, M.a., Xie, H., Zhang, L.: Investigating bisulfite short-read mapping failure with hairpin bisulfite sequencing data. BMC Genomics **16**(11), S2 (2015)
21. Porter, J., Zhang, L.: InfoTrim: A DNA read quality trimmer using entropy. In: 2017 IEEE 7th International Conference on Computational Advances in Bio and Medical Sciences (ICCABS), pp. 1–2. IEEE (2017)
22. Porter, J., Zhang, L.: BisPin and BFAST-Gap: Mapping bisulfite-treated reads, p. 26. bioRxiv (2018). https://doi.org/10.1101/284596, https://www.biorxiv.org/content/early/2018/06/16/284596
23. Quail, M.A., et al.: A tale of three next generation sequencing platforms: comparison of Ion Torrent, Pacific Biosciences and Illumina MiSeq sequencers. BMC Genomics **13**(1), 1–13 (2012)
24. Rougemont, J., Amzallag, A., Iseli, C., Farinelli, L., Xenarios, I., Naef, F.: Probabilistic base calling of Solexa sequencing data. BMC Bioinform. **9**(1), 1–12 (2008)
25. Schmid, C.W., Deininger, P.L.: Sequence organization of the human genome. Cell **6**(3), 345–358 (1975)
26. Shannon, C.E., Weaver, W.: The Mathematical Theory of Communication. University of Illinois Press (1949)
27. Snoek, J., Larochelle, H., Adams, R.P.: Practical Bayesian optimization of machine learning algorithms. In: Advances in Neural Information Processing Systems, pp. 2951–2959 (2012)
28. Starostina, E., Tamazian, G., Dobrynin, P., O'Brien, S., Komissarov, A.: Cookiecutter: a tool for KMER-based read filtering and extraction, p. 024679. bioRxiv (2015)
29. Tran, H., Porter, J., Sun, M.a., Xie, H., Zhang, L.: Objective and comprehensive evaluation of bisulfite short read mapping tools. In: Advances in Bioinformatics, vol. 2014, p. 11 (2014)
30. Wang, X.V., Blades, N., Ding, J., Sultana, R., Parmigiani, G.: Estimation of sequencing error rates in short reads. BMC Bioinform. **13**(1), 185 (2012)
31. Zielezinski, A., Vinga, S., Almeida, J., Karlowski, W.M.: Alignment-free sequence comparison: benefits, applications, and tools. Genome Biol. **18**(1), 186 (2017)
32. Zou, L.S., et al.: BoostMe accurately predicts DNA methylation values in whole-genome bisulfite sequencing of multiple human tissues, p. 207506. bioRxiv (2018)

MetaProb 2: Improving Unsupervised Metagenomic Binning with Efficient Reads Assembly Using Minimizers

F. Andreace, C. Pizzi, and M. Comin[✉]

Department of Information Engineering, University of Padua, 35100 Padua, Italy
{cinzia.pizzi,comin}@dei.unipd.it

Abstract. Current technologies allow the sequencing of microbial communities directly from the environment without prior culturing. One of the major problems when analyzing a microbial sample is to taxonomically annotate its reads to identify the species it contains. Taxonomic analysis of microbial communities requires reads clustering, a process referred to as binning. The major problems of metagenomics reads binning are the lack of taxonomically related genomes in existing reference databases, the uneven abundance ratio of species, and sequencing errors.

In this paper we present MetaProb 2 an unsupervised binning method based on reads assembly and probabilistic k-mers statistics. The novelties of MetaProb 2 are the use of minimizers to efficiently assemble reads into unitigs and a community detection algorithm based on graph modularity to cluster unitigs and to detect representative unitigs. The effectiveness of MetaProb 2 is demonstrated in both simulated and synthetic datasets in comparison with state-of-art binning tools such as MetaProb, AbundanceBin, Bimeta and MetaCluster.

Available at: https://github.com/frankandreace/metaprob2.

Keywords: Metagenomic · Reads binning · Reads assembly with minimizers · k-mers statistics

1 Introduction

Metagenomics is the study of the heterogeneous microbes samples (e.g. soil, water, human microbiome) directly extracted from the natural environment with the primary goal of determining the taxonomical identity of the microorganisms residing in the samples [22]. Shifting the focus from the individual microbe study to a complex microbial community is a revolutionary milestone. The classical genomic-based approaches require the prior clone and culturing for further investigation [5,14]. However, not all bacteria can be cultured. The advent of metagenomics allowed researchers to overcome this difficulty. Microbial communities can be analyzed and compared through the detection and quantification of the species they contain [9,17]. In this paper, we will focus on the unsupervised detection of species in a sample without the use of reference

© Springer Nature Switzerland AG 2021
S. K. Jha et al. (Eds.): ICCABS 2020, LNBI 12686, pp. 15–25, 2021.
https://doi.org/10.1007/978-3-030-79290-9_2

genomes. Despite extensive studies, accurate binning of reads remains challenging [3,20]. Supervised methods require to index a database of reference genomes, e.g. the NCBI/RefSeq databases of bacterial genomes, that is used to classify [15,16,18,21,26]. Although the reads classification is very efficient, the construction of k-mers DB usually is very demanding, requiring computing capabilities with large amounts of RAM and disk space. Another drawback is the fact that most bacteria found in environmental samples are unknown and cannot be cultured and separated in the laboratory [4]. As a consequence, the genomes of most microbes in an environmental sample lack a taxonomically related sequences in existing reference databases. For these reasons, when using supervised methods the number of unassigned reads can be very high [6,12,23].

Unsupervised methods do not require to know all the genomes in the sample, instead they try to divide the reads into groups so that reads from the same species are clustered together. Unsupervised classification tools, also known as binning, are based on the observation that the k-mer distributions of the DNA fragments from the same genome are more similar than those from different genomes. Thus, without using any reference genome, one can determine if two fragments are from genomes of similar species based on their k-mer distributions. The major problem when processing metagenomic data is the fact that the proportion of species in a sample, a.k.a. abundance rate, can vary greatly. Most of the tools can only handle species with even abundance ratios, and their binning performances degrade significantly in real situations when the abundance ratios of the species are different. For example, AbundanceBin [27] works well for very different abundance ratios, but problems arise when some species have similar abundance ratios. Other tools like BiMeta [24] and MetaCluster [25] try to group the reads into many small clusters so that reads from minority species (with low abundance ratios) could exist as isolated clusters. Both these methods use as means of comparison the Euclidean distance between the vectors of k-mers counts on the clusters groups. In MetaProb [8] reads are clustered based on a self-standardized statistic, derived from alignment-free statistics, that is not dominated by the noise in the individual sequences, and that can compare groups of reads with different abundance ratios. The sensitivity can be improved by using spaced seeds instead of k-mers [7], however at the expenses of the computing resources.

In terms of precision Metaprob has shown to be one of the best performing methods, however the major bottleneck is the high memory consumption. Another important observation is that all reads binning methods try to cluster reads, based on overlaps and k-mers counts, but without assembling the reads. A possible explanation is because metagenomics reads assembly is very challenging [20]. However, efficient techniques based on minimizers have been recently devised for long reads mapping and assembly [10,11]. Recently, GraphBin [13] has shown that assembly can be of help also for the problem of contig binning.

In this paper we present MetaProb 2, a new approach to address the problem of unsupervised metagenomics reads binning. To this purpose, MetaProb 2 assembles reads into unitigs using efficient techniques based on minimizers, as well as probabilistic sequence signatures based on k-mers. The use of unitigs will also prevent the overestimation of k-mers frequency, and it does not requires complex counting procedures like finding sets of independent reads as in MetaProb [8]. Another novelty of MetaProb 2 is a community detection algorithm based on graph modularity [2] to cluster unitigs and to detect putative species. This novel paradigm exploited by MetaProb 2 will further improve the classification accuracy while reducing the computational resources (see Sect. 3).

2   Method

The study of DNA based on its k-mers is a well know technique to identify the species in a metagenomic sample. One drawback of this approach is the large amount of memory required to compute reads overlaps and to store all the k-mers of the sequences. In order to solve these issues we propose MetaProb 2, a new metagenomic reads binning algorithm based on minimizers. This algorithm uses short paired-end reads to infer the number of species and the abundance in the sample: short reads provide high accuracy and the paired-end information will be useful to improve the precision and overall performances of the algorithm.

An overview of MetaProb 2 can be found in Fig. 1. The method consists of three main steps. In the first phase, reads are grouped together based on their overlap, using minimizers instead of k-mers. Since these reads share a common subsequence, they are assumed to belong to the same species, and assembled together to generate an unitig, i.e. a precise contig in which the consensus is unambiguous. These operations are performed using two long reads de-novo assembly algorithms, Minimap2 [11] and Miniasm [10], with some additional modifications to comply with the short reads input.

In the second phase a unitig graph is built considering the unitigs - and their associated reads - as nodes. From this graph it is possible to infer communities of nodes that will likely represent unitigs of the same species. The third and last step is the identification of putative species and the estimation of their abundances. In this phase the representative unitigs and the unassembled reads are clustered together based on k-mers content using a probabilistic sequence signature derived from MetaProb [8]. Next, a more detailed description of each of these steps is given.

2.1   Phase 1: Unitig Construction

In the first phase, reads are grouped together, based on their overlaps, and then assembled. This operation is performed using Minimap2 [11], a long-read de novo mapping tool that uses minimizers instead of k-mers to find shared subsequences between reads. The use of minimizers is crucial because it stores only a fraction of all the k-mers to perform the all vs. all comparison between the sequences, resulting in faster computation and lower memory usage. In fact, Minimap2 has the best performances in long reads mapping and assembling. Unlike MetaProb, the k-mer length is set to 15 and not 32, which is a good trade-off between resources usage, precision and number of reads grouped: higher k-mer length means worst performances in computation time, memory usage and grouped

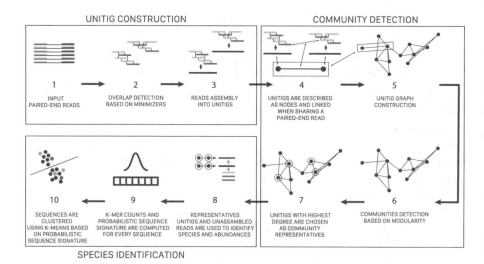

Fig. 1. An overview of MetaProb 2 and the three main phases: Unitig construction, Community detection and Species identification.

reads but it guarantees higher precision. Regarding the window size in which minimizers are chosen we used 10, as the recommended value was 2/3 of the k-mer length [11].

Instead of working on the groups of overlapping reads, we assemble the sequences in each group and we consider the resulting unitig. Unitigs are precise assemblies generated from overlapping sequences: we decided to not combine them together into contigs to preserve the high quality of the assembled reads, since our purpose is to have the more precise information as possible. Moreover, the fact of considering unitigs instead of groups of reads it will naturally resolve the problem of k-mers overcounting, and also it will avoid the complex phase of finding sets of independent reads of MetaProb [8].

The benefit of using minimizers for short reads assembly as been recently shown in [1]. Miniasm [10] is a tool often used together with Minimap2 that performs assembly on long reads, it provides as output the unitig sequences along with other information. As suggested by [1], we change the default parameters of minimap2 and miniasm to accommodate for short reads assembly. Note that not all the reads in the input sample will contribute to the assembly of some unitigs, however they will be considered in the final phase.

2.2   Phase 2: Community Detection

In this phase, we use the information provided by the overlap detection together with the paired-end structure of the reads to group unitigs that are likely to be from the same species. To do so every unitig is assigned to a node in a graph and if two unitigs share part of a paired-end read, their respective nodes are linked together. Every edge is weighted with the number of shared reads between the unitigs. Then we use a graph clustering algorithm on the unitig graph in order to detect the communities of unitigs. Since the dimension of the graph can be large, this operation is performed using an heuristic method based on modularity optimization [2]. This method is extremely efficient both in time and memory and it can handle very large graphs. Moreover, this operation relies on the assumption that unitigs that share many paired-end reads are likely to be originated from the same species. It is important to notice that the communities we obtain are very precise (data not shown), as the reads they contain are almost all from the same species. However, a given community does not necessarily contain all the reads from a species. It may well be that two or more communities are composed by reads of the same species. This calls for an additional step based on the sequence statistics, that will have the specific purpose to detect the real number of species and their abundance in the sample.

Once the communities of unitigs have been created, we selected from every community the nodes with the highest degrees, and these unitigs will be considered as representatives for that community in the last phase. In particular, we chose the nodes with the highest degrees because they will somehow better represent the community while avoiding the possibility of choosing an outlier. In order to limit the number of representative unitigs we set a threshold on the sum of the representative's sequences length. The representative unitigs of each community are used in the last phase in place of all the reads belonging to that community, making the species identification step faster while keeping the sequence information useful to estimate the number of species.

2.3 Phase 3: Species Identification

In the last phase, we infer the number of species and their abundance in the sample from the sequence information, using sequence signatures [8] based on k-mer statistics. Several alignment-free statistics have been proposed over the years [28]. In the context of metagenomic binning, the sequence signatures proposed by MetaProb [8] have shown very good performance and we decided to use the sequence signature for the final phase. The input sequences for the species identification step are the representative unitigs, that account for all the reads in the communities, and the remaining unassembled reads. First we compute the k-mer frequency distribution for each sequence. Then, to account for the different probability of appearance of k-mers, the k-mers counts are standardized based on the probability of k-mers in each sequence. Finally, in order to compare sequences of different length, the sequence signatures are computed for each input string, see [8] for more details. In order to detect sequences that are likely to belong to the same species we evaluate the distance between the sequence signatures and we apply k-means to group sequences with a similar distribution.

3 Results and Discussion

In this section we describe several experiments we performed to assess the performances of MetaProb 2. In particular we measured both the quality of the results, and the computational resource usage in terms of time and space required for the processing. All the experiments were performed on a machine with an Intel Xeon Gold 5118 @2.30 GHz, using 32 cores and 32 GB of RAM. The input parameters for minimap2 are "-X -sc -t31" while for miniasm are "-12 -m1 -o2 -I0.001 -s2 -i0.001 -c1 -e0 -n0 -r0.99,0.01".

3.1   Datasets Description and Performance Evaluation Metrics

We used two different kinds of datasets: ten simulated bacterial metagenomes generated using MetaSim [19], called S1-10, and two containing synthetic metagenomes based on real reads, called MIX1-2. The S1-10 datasets were used in previous studies to assess the performances of BiMeta [24] and MetaProb [8]. Mix1-2 were also used to validate MetaProb.

The S datasets contain short paired-end reads, which length is approximately 80 bp, generated according to the Illumina error profile with an error rate of 1% using MetaSim. These have been used to verify the consistency of this method in different scenarios: from datasets like S1-4 that have only 2 different species and hundreds of thousands of reads with similar abundances to S9-10 that have 15 and 30 number of species, between 2.3 and 5 millions of reads and different abundance ratios and different phylogenetic distance. The synthetic datasets, constructed from real metagenomic data are composed of short reads Illumina MiSeq from Kraken [26] with 10 different species and two abundance profiles: spanning between 3.5 to 5 millions of reads they have been used to validate the quality of the method. Table 1 shows number of reads, species and phylogenetic distance for each dataset.

Table 1. Number of reads, species and phylogenetic distance of each sample.

Dataset	No. of reads	No. of species	Phylogenetic distance
S1	96367	2	Species
S2	195339	2	Species
S3	338725	2	Order
S4	375302	2	Phylum
S5	325400	3	Species and Family
S6	713388	3	Phylum and Kingdom
S7	1653550	5	Genus and Order
S8	456224	5	Genus and Order
S9	2234168	15	various distances
S10	4990632	30	various distances
MIX1	4814943	10	various distances
MIX2	3574950	10	various distances

In order to evaluate the results we used three performance evaluation metrics: precision, recall and f-measure. Given n as number of species in a dataset and C the number of clusters returned by the algorithm, A_{ij} is the number of reads from species j assigned to cluster i. We used the same definitions of precision, recall and f-measure as in MetaProb [8] and BiMeta [24]:

$$Precision = \frac{\sum_{i=1}^{C} \max_j A_{ij}}{\sum_{i=1}^{C} \sum_{j=1}^{n} A_{ij}} \tag{1}$$

$$Recall = \frac{\sum_{j=1}^{n} \max_i A_{ij}}{\sum_{i=1}^{C} \sum_{j=1}^{n} A_{ij} + \#unassigned - reads} \tag{2}$$

$$F - measure = \frac{2 * Precision * Recall}{Precision + Recall} \tag{3}$$

3.2   Results

In this section we discuss the results of the comparison between MetaProb 2 and MetaProb, alongside with other algorithms like MetaCluster 5.0.1 [25], AbundanceBin [27] and BiMeta [24].

Quality of Binning. The ability of MetaProb 2 to perform metagenomic binning is compared against the performances of its predecessor, MetaProb, along with MetaCluster, AbundanceBin and BiMeta. Table 2 shows the overall F-measure values of all the algorithms for each dataset (S1-10, MIX1-2). The data reported for the competitors are also shown in Table 1 of the MetaProb paper [8].

Table 2. The comparison of f-measure for all algorithms on all datasets.

Dataset	Abundance bin	MetaCluster	BiMeta	MetaProb	MetaProb 2
S1	0.683	0.672	0.978	0.992	**0.994**
S2	0.713	0.631	0.581	**0.879**	0.818
S3	0.824	0.415	**0.978**	0.920	0.952
S4	0.883	0.460	0.994	0.916	**0.997**
S5	0.552	0.643	0.690	0.828	**0.880**
S6	0.692	0.492	0.858	0.953	**0.997**
S7	0.606	0.652	**0.843**	0.775	0.816
S8	0.528	0.529	0.743	0.770	**0.834**
S9	Error	0.639	0.791	0.765	**0.842**
S10	0.137	0.052	0.429	0.694	**0.733**
MIX1	0.534	0.555	0.645	**0.737**	0.733
MIX2	0.490	0.630	0.667	0.670	**0.800**
MEAN	0.554	0.531	0.766	0.825	**0.866**

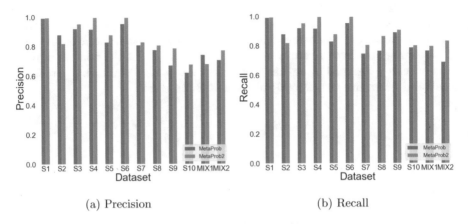

(a) Precision   (b) Recall

Fig. 2. Precision and Recall comparison between MetaProb and MetaProb 2 on all datasets.

We observed that increasing the dataset complexity (number of species, different abundances) results in a decrease of performances for every algorithm. While AbundanceBin and MetaCluster always have lower performances than the others, BiMeta and MetaProb have overall good performances and perform well for specific datasets. MetaProb 2 is the best for 8 out of 12 samples, in particular, it outperforms all the other algorithms on the most difficult datasets (from S8 to MIX2), except for MIX1, where the result is almost equal to MetaProb. It is important to notice that the best improvements in terms of overall binning quality (F-measure) have been made for the most complex datasets. MetaProb 2 F-measure values are between 5% and 15% better than the next best BiMeta and MetaProb.

Precision and Recall Values for MetaProb and MetaProb 2 are shown in details in Fig. 2. Both algorithms have balanced levels of precision and recall in all datasets. MetaProb 2 obtains in most cases a better performance than MetaProb in terms of both precision and recall. Results show very high values even for the realistic datasets (MIX1 and MIX2), and consistent with the most complex among the simulated datasets. These results show that the probabilistic sequence signature introduced in MetaProb is a powerful tool and that the two new phases that have been added in MetaProb 2 strengthens it even further.

Computational Resources. We compared the running time and memory usage of MetaProb and MetaProb 2 to understand to which extent the modifications proposed in this paper affect the computational burden of the process. As shown in Fig. 3, MetaProb 2 outperforms MetaProb, showing less computational time and significantly lower memory usage.

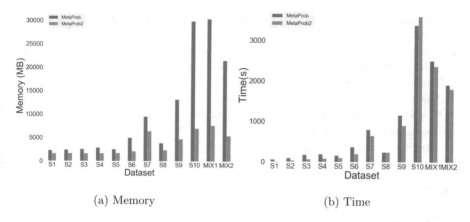

(a) Memory   (b) Time

Fig. 3. Time and Memory comparison between MetaProb and MetaProb 2.

Processing time was not considered an issue. As shown in the MetaProb paper [8], it was already an order of magnitude faster than AbundanceBin and BiMeta, while it was comparable to MetaCluster. Nevertheless, MetaProb 2 is faster on almost every dataset: this has been possible since reads assembly using minimizer is a fast operation, and the graph clustering algorithm scales well with the dimension of the dataset. Moreover, these results can be further improved, since some operations in the second phase are still done on a single core and cannot exploit multicore processing.

On the other hand, the heavy memory usage of MetaProb was the driving factor for the development of a new approach. Even if the performances of MetaProb are good, the amount of RAM used is higher than the other algorithms. For example, both AbundanceBin and MetaCluster memory usage are better than MetaProb, while BiMeta is in line with MetaProb.

As shown in Fig. 3, MetaProb 2 consistently uses less memory than its predecessor, requiring significantly less space as the size of the dataset grows. For example on the largest dataset with 5 million reads MetaProb requires 30.4 GB of RAM while MetaProb 2 only 7.6 GB, with a reduction of 75%, in line with AbundanceBin that uses 5.7 GB.

These results have been possible thanks to the use of minimizers that considerably reduce the number of k-mers stored for the overlap detection. Also, the efficient unitig graph algorithms, and the resulting smaller number of sequences to compare, make then possible to keep the memory usage low: in fact, the highest amount of memory usage is always registered in the first phase.

4   Conclusions and Future Work

Binning metagenomic reads remains a crucial step in metagenomic analysis. In this work we presented MetaProb 2, an unsupervised approach for metagenomic reads binning based on reads assembly using minimizers and on probabilistic k-mers statistics. We compared the binning performance over simulated and synthetic metagenomic datasets against other state-of-art binning algorithms. MetaProb 2 achieves good performances in terms of precision and recall, outperforming MetaProb and the other tools. Another advantage of MetaProb 2 is the small memory requirement, especially on large dataset, with a reduction of 75% w.r.t. to MetaProb. As future work we will expand the experimental setup with even larger datasets, we will test other metagenomic assemblers, as in GraphBin [13], and we plan to develop a similar paradigm for the problem of taxonomic reads annotation.

References

1. Bayat, A., Deshpande, N.P., Wilkins, M.R., Parameswaran, S.: Fast short read de-novo assembly using overlap-layout-consensus approach. IEEE/ACM Trans. Comput. Biol. Bioinform. **17**(01), 334–338 (2020). https://doi.org/10.1109/TCBB.2018.2875479

2. Blondel, V.D., Guillaume, J.L., Lambiotte, R., Lefebvre, E.: Fast unfolding of communities in large networks. J. Stat. Mech. Theory Experiment **2008**(10), P10008 (2008). https://doi.org/10.1088/1742-5468/2008/10/p10008

3. Comin, M., Di Camillo, B., Pizzi, C., Vandin, F.: Comparison of microbiome samples: methods and computational challenges. Briefings Bioinform. **22**, 88 (2020). https://doi.org/10.1093/bib/bbaa121

4. Eisen, J.A.: Environmental shotgun sequencing its potential and challenges for studying the hidden world of microbes. PLoS Biol. **5**, e82 (2007)

5. Felczykowska, A., Bloch, S.K., Nejman-Faleńczyk, B., Barańska, S.: Metagenomic approach in the investigation of new bioactive compounds in the marine environment. Acta Biochimica Polonica **59**(4), 501–505 (2012)

6. Girotto, S., Comin, M., Pizzi, C.: Higher recall in metagenomic sequence classification exploiting overlapping reads. BMC Genomics **18**(10), 917 (2017)

7. Girotto, S., Comin, M., Pizzi, C.: Metagenomic reads binning with spaced seeds. In: Theoretical Computer Science, Algorithms, Strings and Theoretical Approaches in the Big Data Era (In Honor of the 60th Birthday of Professor Raffaele Giancarlo), vol. 698, pp. 88–99 (2017). https://doi.org/10.1016/j.tcs.2017.05.023

8. Girotto, S., Pizzi, C., Comin, M.: Metaprob: accurate metagenomic reads binning based on probabilistic sequence signatures. Bioinformatics **32**(17), i567–i575 (2016). https://doi.org/10.1093/bioinformatics/btw466

9. Kang, D.D., Froula, J., Egan, R., Wang, Z.: MetaBAT: an efficient tool for accurately reconstructing single genomes from complex microbial communities. PeerJ **3**, e1165 (2015). https://doi.org/10.7717/peerj.1165

10. Li, H.: Minimap and miniasm: fast mapping and de novo assembly for noisy long sequences. Bioinformatics **32**(14), 2103–2110 (2016). https://doi.org/10.1093/bioinformatics/btw152

11. Li, H.: Minimap2: pairwise alignment for nucleotide sequences. Bioinformatics **34**(18), 3094–3100 (2018). https://doi.org/10.1093/bioinformatics/bty191

12. Lindgreen, S., Adair, K., Gardner, P.: An Evaluation of the Accuracy and Speed of Metagenome Analysis Tools. Cold Spring Harbor Laboratory Press, Woodbury (2015)

13. Mallawaarachchi, V., Wickramarachchi, A., Lin, Y.: GraphBin: refined binning of metagenomic contigs using assembly graphs. Bioinformatics **36**(11), 3307–3313 (2020)
14. Mande, S.S., Mohammed, M.H., Ghosh, T.S.: Classification of metagenomic sequences: methods and challenges. Briefings Bioinform. **13**(6), 669–681 (2012). https://doi.org/10.1093/bib/bbs054
15. Marchiori, D., Comin, M.: SKraken: fast and sensitive classification of short metagenomic reads based on filtering uninformative k-mers. In: BIOINFORMAT-ICS 2017–8th International Conference on Bioinformatics Models, Methods and Algorithms, Proceedings; Part of 10th International Joint Conference on Biomedical Engineering Systems and Technologies, BIOSTEC 2017, vol. 3, pp. 59–67 (2017)
16. Ounit, R., Wanamaker, S., Close, T.J., Lonardi, S.: CLARK: fast and accurate classification of metagenomic and genomic sequences using discriminative k-mers. BMC Genomics **16**(1), 1–13 (2015)
17. Qian, J., Comin, M.: MetaCon: unsupervised clustering of metagenomic contigs with probabilistic k-mers statistics and coverage. BMC Bioinform. **20**(367), 1–12 (2019). https://doi.org/10.1186/s12859-019-2904-4
18. Qian, J., Marchiori, D., Comin, M.: Fast and sensitive classification of short metagenomic reads with SKraken. In: Peixoto, N., Silveira, M., Ali, H.H., Maciel, C., van den Broek, E.L. (eds.) BIOSTEC 2017. CCIS, vol. 881, pp. 212–226. Springer, Cham (2018). https://doi.org/10.1007/978-3-319-94806-5_12
19. Richter, D., Ott, F., Auch, A., Schmid, R., Huson, D.: MetaSim-a sequencing simulator for genomics and metagenomics. PloS One **3**, e3373 (2008). https://doi.org/10.1371/journal.pone.0003373
20. Sczyrba, A., Hofmann, P., McHardy, A.C.: Critical assessment of metagenome interpretation-a benchmark of metagenomics software. Nat. Methods **14**, 1063–1071 (2017)
21. Segata, N., Waldron, L., Ballarini, A., Narasimhan, V., Jousson, O., Huttenhower, C.: Metagenomic microbial community profiling using unique clade-specific marker genes. Nat. Methods **9**, 811 (2012)
22. Staley, J.T., Konopka, A.: Measurement of in situ activities of nonphotosynthetic microorganisms in aquatic and terrestrial habitats. Ann. Rev. Microbiol. **39**(1), 321–346 (1985). https://doi.org/10.1146/annurev.mi.39.100185.001541. pMID: 3904603
23. Storato, D., Comin, M.: Improving metagenomic classification using discriminative k-mers from sequencing data. In: Cai, Z., Mandoiu, I., Narasimhan, G., Skums, P., Guo, X. (eds.) ISBRA 2020. LNCS, vol. 12304, pp. 68–81. Springer, Cham (2020). https://doi.org/10.1007/978-3-030-57821-3_7
24. Vinh, L.V., Lang, T.V., Binh, L.T., Hoai, T.V.: A two-phase binning algorithm using l-mer frequency on groups of non-overlapping reads. Algorithms Mol. Biol. **10**(1), 1–12 (2015). https://doi.org/10.1186/s13015-014-0030-4
25. Wang, Y., Leung, H.C., Yiu, S.M., Chin, F.Y.: MetaCluster 5.0: a two-round binning approach for metagenomic data for low-abundance species in a noisy sample. Bioinform. **28**, i356 (2012). https://doi.org/10.1093/bioinformatics/bts397
26. Wood, D., Salzberg, S.: Kraken: ultrafast metagenomic sequence classification using exact alignments. Genome Biol. **15**, 1–12 (2014)
27. Wu, Y.W., Ye, Y.: A novel abundance-based algorithm for binning metagenomic sequences using l-tuples. J. Comput. Biol. **18**, 523 (2011). https://doi.org/10.1089/cmb.2010.0245
28. Zielezinski, A., Girgis, H., Bernard, G., et al.: Benchmarking of alignment-free sequence comparison methods. Genome Biol. **20**(1), 144 (2019)

Computational Study of Action Potential Generation in Urethral Smooth Muscle Cell

Chitaranjan Mahapatra$^{(\boxtimes)}$

Cardiovascular Research Institute,
University of California San Francisco, San Francisco 94158, USA
chitaranjan.mahapatra@ucsf.edu

Abstract. Stress urinary incontinence is defined by the involuntary loss of urine during the sneezing and coughing. The urethral smooth muscle cell contributes to stress urinary incontinence by generating spontaneous mechanical and electrical activities. It generates spontaneous electrical events in the terms of membrane depolarization and action potentials. Therefore, a complete understanding of the urethral smooth muscle cell's spontaneous action potential biophysics will help in identifying novel pharmacological targets for the stress urinary incontinence. The action potential is evoked by the activation of various ion channels across the cell membrane. This study aims in establishing a computational model of the single urethral smooth muscle cell to simulate the action potential after incorporating all-important ion channels. The ion channels are designed with Hodgkin- Huxley formalism, where the internal kinetics are expressed in terms of the ordinary differential equations. This computational model generates experimental spontaneous action potential and the underlying ionic currents in urethral smooth muscle cell successfully. In summary, this mathematical model contributes an elemental tool to investigate the physiological ionic mechanisms underlying the spikes in the urethral smooth muscle cell, which in turn can shed light on the genesis of stress urinary incontinence.

Keywords: Stress urinary incontinence · Urethral smooth muscle cell · Action potential · Ion channels · Computational modeling

1 Introduction

The International Continence Society has defined urinary incontinence (UI) as a condition in which involuntary loss of urine is objectively demonstrable and is a social or hygiene problem [1]. Among different types of UI, stress urinary incontinence (SUI) is one, which is a common syndrome in women that is typically associated with advanced age, obesity, diabetes mellitus, and fertility [2]. Stress urinary incontinence, defined as a "complaint of involuntary loss of urine on effort or physical exertion or on sneezing or coughing" by the International Continence Society [3, 4]. The smooth muscles from the urinary bladder and urethra display spontaneous contractility patterns, which are associated with UI and SUI. The mammalian urethra is known to exhibit spontaneous tonic contraction activity during the urine-storage phase [5]. Although the factors regulating

© Springer Nature Switzerland AG 2021
S. K. Jha et al. (Eds.): ICCABS 2020, LNBI 12686, pp. 26–32, 2021.
https://doi.org/10.1007/978-3-030-79290-9_3

the SUI are not still precisely identified, it is also widely demonstrated that the abnormal urethral smooth muscle (USM) cell contraction phenomena play an important role in regulating these activities [6–8]. The isolated USM cell from various species shows slow waves, spontaneous depolarization (SD), and spontaneous action potentials (sAPs) as its' intracellular electrical activity [7, 9, 10]. The sAPs trigger spontaneous contractions by permitting extracellular calcium (Ca^{2+}) via the voltage gated Ca^{2+} channels across the membrane and releasing stored Ca^{2+} from the sarcoplasmic reticulum (SR) in the intracellular compartment [5, 10, 11]. The resting membrane potential (RMP) values of the USM cell are in the range from -35 mV to -45 mV [12–14]. The sAPs can be fired spontaneously or evoked by the external stimulation [13]. The array of ion channels located across the USM cell membrane play a crucial role in regulating both RMP and sAP formation and therefore the overall function of the urethra [15]. Therefore, a better understanding of the ion channel kinetics in forming the USM cell sAP would shed light on developing improved therapies for the SUI.

The biophysical constrained computational models always provide a virtual experimental set up to investigate the underlying ionic mechanisms for the cell's electrical activities. Over the past decades, several computational models have been developed for the neuronal and cardiac cells to investigate individual ion channels' contribution in generating the action potential. However, there are a few numbers of computational models are developed for smooth muscle electrophysiology. To address this gap, recently, we have developed a biophysically constrained computational model for the detrusor smooth muscle (DSM) AP by incorporating nine ion channels [16–19]. As both DSM and USM contractions are related to UI and SUI, this paper presents the first biophysically based model of USM AP which integrates some ionic currents underlying the electrogenic processes in the urethra. This single-cell USM model can be subsequently coupled to other active ionic currents and a syncytium model to examine hypotheses concerning the generation of SUI.

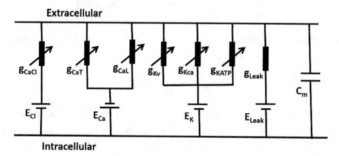

Fig. 1. A USM cell parallel conductance model. It describes all membrane currents and transmembrane potential.

2 Methods

The first step in developing this computational model is to form a conceptual model expressed by the mathematical equations. The classical Hodgkin-Huxley (HH) approach is implemented to form this conceptual model. According to the HH formalism, the cell membrane can be interpreted into an equivalent parallel conductance circuit consisting of membrane capacitance and several variable conductances representing all ion channels. The USM cell model simulation is performed in "NEURON" [20] software environment. The "NEURON" simulation platform is designed to investigate electrophysiological properties in biological excitable cells at different spatiotemporal levels. For USM cell geometry, a cylindrical morphology is considered with length and diameter of 200 μm and 6 μm respectively. The membrane capacitance (C_m), membrane resistance (R_m), and axial resistance (R_a) are basic electrical properties of the excitable cell membrane. For this model, the C_m, R_m, and R_a are taken as 1 μF/cm^2, 138 MΩ–cm^2, and 181 Ω-cm respectively. Figure 1 illustrates the USM cell model as a parallel conductance model. The membrane capacitance (C_m) is shunted by an array of ion channel conductances g_{ion} with respective Nernst potentials E_{ion}. The ion channels in the USM cell model are Ca^{2+} activated Cl$^-$ channel (g_{CaCl}, E_{Cl}), voltage-gated Ca^{2+} channel (g_{CaL}, g_{CaT}, E_{Ca}), voltage-gated K$^+$ channel (g_{Kv}, E_K), Ca^{2+} activated K$^+$ channel(g_{Kca}, E_K), ATP-dependent K$^+$ channel (g_{KATP}, E_K) and leakage currents (g_{Leak}, E_{Leak}). The leakage current is considered as a constant value. Applying Kirchhoff's current law, we will get the following differential equation describing changes in transmembrane potential V_m. The time dependence of the membrane potential is governed by the following differential equation

$$\frac{dV_m}{dt} = -\frac{I_{ion(t)}}{C_m} \tag{1}$$

where both V_m, and I_{ion} represent the transmembrane potential and sum of the ionic currents across the cell membrane. The units of both V_m and I_{ion} are in mV and pA respectively.

$$\frac{dV_m}{dt} = -\frac{1}{C_m}(I_{Ca} + I_{KCa} + I_{Kv} + I_l) \tag{2}$$

All ionic currents were modeled according to the Hodgkin-Huxley formalism, which is expressed by the following equation.

$$I = \bar{g}m^x h^y (V_m - E_{rev}) \tag{3}$$

where $\bar{g}$ is the maximum conductance, E_{rev} is the ion's Nernst/reversal potential, m and h are the dimensionless activation and inactivation gating variables.

Both m and h are dependent upon membrane potential and time. First order differential equations are used to express the time dependent properties of both m and h. The following differential equation represents the dynamics of 'm' variable.

$$\frac{dm}{dt} = \frac{(m_\infty - m)}{\tau_m} \tag{4}$$

where m_∞ is the steady-state value of the m and τ_m, is the time constant for reaching the steady-state value. These are also functions of voltage and/or ionic concentrations.

In addition, the steady-state inactivation and activation values for all ion channels are described by the following Boltzman equation.

$$m_\infty = {}^1\!/_1 + \exp\left((V_m + V_{\frac{1}{2}})/s\right) \qquad (5)$$

Where $V_{1/2}$ is the half activation potential and S is the slope factor. For our model, both $V_{1/2}$ and S are taken from the published experimental data.

The sAPs were induced in the whole-cell model by applying an external stimulus current as brief rectangular pulses or synaptic input.

3 Results

There is an array of ion channels discovered in USM cell electrophysiology to regulate the cell's excitability. It includes T and L-type voltage-gated Ca^{2+} channels (I_{CaL} and I_{CaT}), ATP-dependent K^+ channel (I_{KATP}), two outward rectifying voltage-gated K^+ channel (I_{KA} and I_{Kv}), Ca^{2+}, and voltage-dependent large-conductance K^+ channel (I_{KCa}), Ca^{2+} dependent Cl^- channel (I_{ClCa}) and the leakage channel (I_{Leak}). The biophysical details of one inward current (I_{CaL}) is presented in the following section.

L-type Calcium Current (I_{CaL})
Several researcher groups have elucidated the presence of two types of Ca^{2+} channel (Transient and long-lasting type) in USM cell electrophysiology. However, the L-type (Long-lasting) Ca^{2+} channel (I_{CaL}) is responsible for the major inward current in USM cells [5, 15]. It is demonstrated that I_{CaL} is activated first between $V_m \approx -35$ and -20 mV; the peak magnitude of the current-voltage (I–V) relationship curve appears at $V_m \approx 10$mV. The half-activation potentials for both steady-state activation and inactivation curve are –3.4 mV and –24.8 mV respectively. The Nerst potential E_{CaL} is fixed at 45mV. The equations of I_{CaL} incorporate both activation (m) and inactivation (h) gating variables. The biophysical parameters for the I_{CaL} are extracted from the published experimental data in human USM electrophysiology [21]. Figure 2(A) shows the steady-state activation and inactivation curve with respect to membrane potential.

The red and black solid lines represent simulated steady-state curves for inactivation and activation parameters respectively. The superimposed filled squares and triangles represent the experimental data [21]. The whole-cell current I_{CaL} is simulated according to the voltage clamp protocol for a duration of 200 ms. The holding potential is –70 mV. Simulated tracings of I_{CaL} are shown in Fig. 2(B).

AP Simulation
The AP can be evoked either by the external current injection via the inserted electrode or by the induced synaptic input from the neighbor nerve. Seven numbers of ionic conductances are incorporated into this single USM cell model. The USM cell model successfully responded to both current and synaptic input stimuli by showing all-or-none AP firing properties.

A current input is a step input pulse with different amplitudes and durations. A synaptic input is also mimicked by the alpha function to evoke AP in our model. The

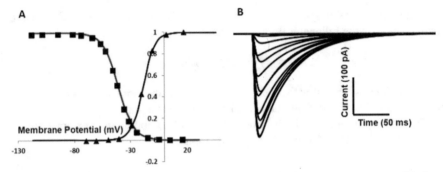

Fig. 2. USM I_{CaL} model. A steady state activation and inactivation parameter curve and B shows the current traces from the voltage clamp protocol.

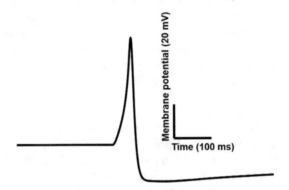

Fig. 3. The simulated AP in the USM model.

voltage threshold is ≈ -35 mV. Figure 3 presents the simulated AP after inducing a synaptic input to mimic the experimental AP in [22].

Table 1 compares simulated AP with experimental one [22] in terms of RMP, peak amplitude, AP duration and AHP (after hyperpolarization potential).

Table 1. Comparison between simulated AP and the experimental AP [22]

	RMP (mV)	Peak (mV)	AHP (mV)	Duration (ms)
Experiment	–40	47	–53	38
Simulation	–40	55	–52	35

4   Discussion

The primary objective of this study was to develop and validate a computational model of a USM cellular electrophysiology. The model description integrates those ion channels that were significantly contributing to generate the USM cell AP. The ion channel kinetics are characterized by the Hodgkin and Huxley formalism after extracting all parameter values from the literature on USM electrophysiology. The model has demonstrated its' ability by simulating the experimental AP successfully.

The assumptions and simplification approaches are concerned about developing a perfect mathematical model.

A better physiologically realistic model is always based on enough electrophysiological data obtained from a single species. However, due to experimental setup complexity, these data are not always available from the same species. We, therefore, made assumptions driven from values obtained from USM in different species (rat, human, mouse, pig, guinea pig, and rabbit) and under various experimental conditions. Some debate also exists with regard to the ionic conductances that are involved in the repolarizing phase. It has been suggested that more than one K^+ conductance (for example fast A-type K^+ current [15] may carry a portion of the outward current. However, due to a lack of experimental evidence, this model doesn't include this channel. Another question can also be raised towards simulating the experimental AP when the single USM cell is coupled to the other cell.

In the present state, this model is at an elementary stage. Integration of other active channels, Na^+- Ca^{2+} exchanger, Ca^{2+} ATPase pump and sarcoplasmic reticulum Ca^{2+} releasing mechanism will improve this model towards a more comprehensive stage. In addition, the expansion of this single-cell model to syncytium or network level will help to establish a better physiologically realistic computational model for investigating the SUI.

References

1. Abrams, P., et al.: The standardisation of terminology in lower urinary tract function: report from the standardisation sub-committee of the International Continence Society. Urology **61**(1), 37–49 (2003)
2. Chen, D., et al.: ANO1 in urethral SMCs contributes to sex differences in urethral spontaneous tone. Am. J. Physiol. Renal Physiol. **319**(3), F394-402 (2020)
3. Chancellor, M.B., Yoshimura, N.: Neurophysiology of stress urinary incontinence. Rev. Urol. **6**(3), S19 (2004)
4. Yono, M., Irie, S., Gotoh, M.: TAS-303 effects on urethral sphincter function in women with stress urinary incontinence: phase I study. Int. Urogynecol. J. **32**(3), 673–680 (2020). https://doi.org/10.1007/s00192-020-04470-7
5. Brading, A.F.: Spontaneous activity of lower urinary tract smooth muscles: correlation between ion channels and tissue function. J. Physiol. **570**(1), 13–22 (2006)
6. Greenland, J.E., Dass, N., Brading, A.F.: Intrinsic urethral closure mechanisms in the female pig. Scand. J. Urol. Nephrol. Supplementum. **179**, 75 (1996)
7. Hollywood, M.A., McCloskey, K.D., McHale, N.G., Thornbury, K.D.: Characterization of outward K+ currents in isolated smooth muscle cells from sheep urethra. Am. J. Physiol. Cell Physiol. **279**(2), C420–C428 (2000)
8. Feng, M., et al.: The RyR–ClCa–VDCC axis contributes to spontaneous tone in urethral smooth muscle. J. Cell. Physiol. **234**(12), 23256–23267 (2019)
9. Hashitani, H., Van Helden, D.F., Suzuki, H.: Properties of spontaneous depolarizations in circular smooth muscle cells of rabbit urethra. Br. J. Pharmacol. **118**(7), 1627 (1996)

10. Hashitani, H., Edwards, F.R.: Spontaneous and neurally activated depolarizations in smooth muscle cells of the guinea-pig urethra. J. Physiol. **514**(2), 459–470 (1999)
11. Berridge, M.J.: Smooth muscle cell calcium activation mechanisms. J. Physiol. **586**(21), 5047–5061 (2008)
12. Teramoto, N., Creed, K.E., Brading, A.F.: Activity of glibenclamide-sensitive K+ channels under unstimulated conditions in smooth muscle cells of pig proximal urethra. Naunyn Schmiedebergs Arch. Pharmacol. **356**(3), 418–424 (1997)
13. Creed, K.E., Oike, M., Ito, Y.: The electrical properties and responses to nerve stimulation of the proximal urethra of the male rabbit. Br. J. Urol. **79**(4), 543–553 (1997)
14. Hashitani, H., Suzuki, H.: Properties of spontaneous Ca2+ transients recorded from interstitial cells of Cajal-like cells of the rabbit urethra in situ. J. Physiol. **583**(2), 505–519 (2007)
15. Kyle, B.D.: Ion channels of the mammalian urethra. Channels **8**(5), 393–401 (2014)
16. Mahapatra, C., Brain, K.L., Manchanda, R.: Computational study of Hodgkin-Huxley type calcium-dependent potassium current in urinary bladder over activity. In: 2018 IEEE 8th International Conference on Computational Advances in Bio and Medical Sciences (ICCABS), pp. 1–4. IEEE (2018)
17. Mahapatra, C., Brain, K.L., Manchanda, R.: A biophysically constrained computational model of the action potential of mouse urinary bladder smooth muscle. PLoS ONE **13**(7), e0200712 (2018)
18. Mahapatra, C., Brain, K.L., Manchanda, R.: Computational studies on urinary bladder smooth muscle: modeling ion channels and their role in generating electrical activity. In: 2015 7th International IEEE/EMBS Conference on Neural Engineering (NER), pp. 832–835. IEEE (2015)
19. Mahapatra, C., Manchanda, R.: Simulation of in vitro-like electrical activities in urinary bladder smooth muscle cells. J. Biomimetics, Biomaterials Biomed. Eng. **33**, 45–51 (2017)
20. Hines, M.L., Carnevale, N.T.: The NEURON simulation environment, neural computation
21. Hollywood, M.A., Woolsey, S., Walsh, I.K., Keane, P.F., McHale, N.G., Thornbury, K.D.: T-and L-type Ca2+ currents in freshly dispersed smooth muscle cells from the human proximal urethra. J. Physiol. **550**(3), 753–764 (2003)
22. Kyle, B., et al.: Contribution of Kv2.1 channels to the delayed rectifier current in freshly dispersed smooth muscle cells from rabbit urethra. Am. J. Physiol. Cell Physiol. **301**(5), C1186-200 (2011)

Metabolic Pathway Prediction using Non-negative Matrix Factorization with Improved Precision

Abdur Rahman Mohd Abul Basher[1] (ID), Ryan J. McLaughlin[1] (ID),
and Steven J. Hallam[1,2(✉)] (ID)

[1] Graduate Program in Bioinformatics, University of British Columbia,
Vancouver, BC V5Z 4S6, Canada
{arbasher,mclaughlinr2}@alumni.ubc.ca
[2] Department of Microbiology and Immunology, University of British Columbia,
Vancouver, BC V6T 1Z3, Canada
shallam@mail.ubc.ca

Abstract. Machine learning provides a probabilistic framework for metabolic pathway inference from genomic sequence information at different levels of complexity and completion. However, several challenges including pathway features engineering, multiple mapping of enzymatic reactions and emergent or distributed metabolism within populations or communities of cells can limit prediction performance. In this paper, we present triUMPF, triple non-negative matrix factorization (NMF) with community detection for metabolic pathway inference, that combines three stages of NMF to capture myriad relationships between enzymes and pathways within a graph network. This is followed by community detection to extract higher order structure based on the clustering of vertices which share similar statistical properties. We evaluated triUMPF performance using experimental datasets manifesting diverse multi-label properties, including Tier 1 genomes from the BioCyc collection of organismal Pathway/Genome Databases and low complexity microbial communities. Resulting performance metrics equaled or exceeded other prediction methods on organismal genomes with improved precision on multi-organismal datasets.

Keywords: NMF · Community detection · Metabolic pathway prediction · MinPath · mlLGPR · MetaCyc · pathway2vec · PathoLogic

1 Introduction

Pathway reconstruction from genomic sequence information is an essential step in describing the metabolic potential of cells at the individual, population and

This work was performed under the auspices Genome Canada, Genome British Columbia, the Natural Sciences and Engineering Research Council (NSERC) of Canada, and Compute/Calcul Canada. ARMAB and RM were supported by UBC four-year doctoral fellowships (4YF) administered through the UBC Graduate Program in Bioinformatics.

© Springer Nature Switzerland AG 2021
S. K. Jha et al. (Eds.): ICCABS 2020, LNBI 12686, pp. 33–44, 2021.
https://doi.org/10.1007/978-3-030-79290-9_4

community levels of biological organization [10,15,20]. Resulting pathway representations provide a foundation for defining regulatory processes, modeling metabolite flux and engineering cells and cellular consortia for defined process outcomes [9,17]. The integral nature of the pathway prediction problem has prompted both gene-centric e.g. mapping annotated proteins onto known pathways using a reference database based on sequence homology, and heuristic or rule-based pathway-centric approaches including PathoLogic [14] and Min-Path [33]. In parallel, the development of trusted sources of curated metabolic pathway information including the Kyoto Encyclopedia of Genes and Genomes (KEGG) [13] and MetaCyc [4] provides training data for the design of more flexible machine learning (ML) algorithms for pathway inference. While ML approaches have been adopted widely in metabolomics research [3,30] they have gained less traction when applied to predicting pathways directly from annotated gene lists.

Dale and colleagues conducted the first in-depth exploration of ML approaches for pathway prediction using Tier 1 (T1) organismal Pathway/Genome Databases (PGDB) [5] from the BioCyc collection randomly divided into training and test sets [6]. Features were developed based on rule-sets used by the PathoLogic algorithm in Pathway Tools to construct PGDBs [14]. Resulting performance metrics indicated that standard ML approaches rivaled PathoLogic performance with the added benefit of probability scores [6]. More recently Basher and colleagues developed multi-label based on logistic regression for pathway prediction (mlLGPR), a multi-label classification approach that uses logistic regression and feature vectors inspired by the work of Dale and colleagues to predict metabolic pathways from genomic sequence information at different levels of complexity and completion [20].

Although mlLGPR performed effectively on organismal genomes, pathway prediction outcomes for multi-organismal datasets were less optimal due in part to missing or noisy feature information. In an effort to solve this problem, Basher and Hallam evaluated the use of representational learning methods to learn a neural embedding-based low-dimensional space of metabolic features based on a three-layered network architecture consisting of compounds, enzymes, and pathways [19]. Learned feature vectors improved pathway prediction performance on organismal genomes and motivated the use of graphical models for multi-organismal features engineering.

Here we describe triple non-negative matrix factorization (NMF) with community detection for metabolic pathway inference (triUMPF) combining three stages of NMF to capture relationships between enzymes and pathways within a network [8] followed by community detection to extract higher order network structure [7]. Non-negative matrix factorization is a data reduction and exploration method in which the original and factorized matrices have the property of non-negative elements with reduced ranks or features [8]. In contrast to other dimension reduction methods, such as principal component analysis [2], NMF both reduces the number of features and preserves information needed to reconstruct the original data [32]. This has important implications for noise robust feature extraction from sparse matrices including datasets associated with gene expression analysis and pathway prediction [32].

For pathway prediction, triUMPF uses three graphs, one representing associations between pathways and enzymes indicated by enzyme commission (EC) numbers [1], one representing interactions between enzymes and another representing interactions between pathways. The two interaction graphs adopt the *subnetworks* concept introduced in BiomeNet [28] and MetaNetSim [12], where a subnetwork is a linked series of connected nodes (e.g. reactions and pathways). In the literature, a subnetwork is commonly referred to as a *community* [26], which defines a set of densely connected nodes within a subnetwork. It is important to emphasize that unless otherwise indicated, the use of the term community in this work refers to a subnetwork community based on statistical properties of a network rather than a community of organisms. Community detection is performed on both interaction graphs (pathways and enzymes) to identify subnetworks among pathways.

We evaluated triUMPF's prediction performance in relation to other methods including MinPath, PathoLogic, and mlLGPR on a set of T1 PGDBs, low complexity microbial communities including symbiont genomes encoding distributed metabolic pathways for amino acid biosynthesis [22], genomes used in the Critical Assessment of Metagenome Interpretation (CAMI) initiative [27], and whole genome shotgun sequences from the Hawaii Ocean Time Series (HOTS) [29] following information hierarchy-based benchmarks initially developed for mlLGPR enabling more robust comparison between pathway prediction methods [20].

2   Method

In this section, we provide a general description of triUMPF components, presented in Fig. 1. At the very beginning, MetaCyc is applied to: i) - extract three association matrices, indicated in step Fig. 1(a), one representing associations between pathways and enzymes (P2E) indicated by enzyme commission (EC) numbers [23], one representing interactions between enzymes (E2E) and another representing interactions between pathways (P2P), and ii) - automatically generate features corresponding pathways and enzymes (or EC) from pathway2vec [19] in Fig. 1(b). Then, triUMPF is trained in two phases: i) - decomposition of the pathway EC association matrix in Fig. 1(c), and ii) - subnetwork or community reconstruction while, simultaneously, learning optimal multi-label pathway parameters in Figs. 1(d–f). Below, we discuss these two phases while the analytical expressions of triUMPF are explained in Appx. Sections A, B, and C [21].

2.1   Decomposing the Pathway EC Association Matrix

Inspired by the idea of non-negative matrix factorization (NMF), we decompose the P2E association matrix to recover low-dimensional latent factor matrices [8]. Unlike previous application of NMF to biological data [24], triUMPF incorporates constraints into the matrix decomposition process. Formally, let $\mathbf{M} \in \mathbb{Z}_{\geq 0}^{t \times r}$

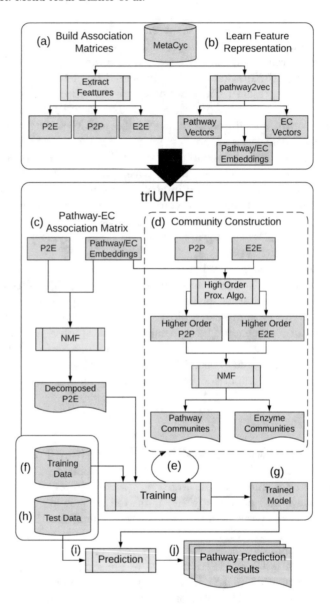

Fig. 1. A workflow diagram showing the proposed triUMPF method. Initially, tri-UMPF takes the Pathway-EC association (P2E) information (a) to produce several low rank matrices (c) while, simultaneously, detecting pathway and EC communities (d) given two interaction matrices, corresponding Pathway-Pathway (P2P) and EC-EC (E2E) (a). For both steps (c) and (d), pathway and EC features obtained from pathway2vec package (b) are utilized. Afterwards, triUMPF iterates between updating community parameters (d) and optimizing multi-label parameters (e) with the use of a training data (f). Once the training is achieved the learned model (g) can be used to predict a set of pathways (i–j) from a newly annotated genome or multi-organismal dataset (h).

be a non-negative matrix, where t is the number of pathways and r is the number of enzymatic reactions. Each row in $\mathbf{M}$ corresponds to a pathway and each column represent an EC, such that $\mathbf{M}_{i,j} = 1$ if an EC j is in pathway i and 0 otherwise. Given $\mathbf{M}$, the standard NMF decomposes this matrix into the two low-rank matrices, i.e. $\mathbf{M} \approx \mathbf{W}\mathbf{H}^{\top}$, where $\mathbf{W} \in \mathbb{R}^{t \times k}$ stores the latent factors for pathways while $\mathbf{H} \in \mathbb{R}^{r \times k}$ is latent factors associated with ECs and $k(\in \mathbb{Z}_{\geq 1}) \ll t, r$. However, triUMPF extends this standard NMF by leveraging features, obtained from *pathway2vec* [19], encoding two interactions: i) - within ECs or pathways and ii) - between pathways and ECs. For more details about this step, please see Appx. Section B.1 [21].

2.2 Community Reconstruction and Multi-label Learning

The community detection problem [18,26] is the task of discovering distinct groups of nodes that are densely connected. During this phase, triUMPF performs community detection to guide the learning process for pathways using binary P2P ($\mathbf{A} \in \mathbb{Z}_{\geq 0}^{t \times t}$) and E2E ($\mathbf{B} \in \mathbb{Z}_{\geq 0}^{r \times r}$) associations matrices, where each entry in these matrices is a binary value indicating an interaction among corresponding entities. However, $\mathbf{A}$ and $\mathbf{B}$ capture pairwise first-order proximity among their related entities, consequently, they are inadequate to fully characterize distant relationships among pathways or ECs [26]. Therefore, triUMPF utilizes higher-order proximity using the following formula [18]:

$$\mathbf{A}^{\mathbf{prox}} = \sum_{i \in l_p} \omega_i \mathbf{A}^l, \qquad \mathbf{B}^{\mathbf{prox}} = \sum_{i \in l_e} \gamma_i \mathbf{B}^l \qquad (1)$$

where $\mathbf{A}^{\mathbf{prox}}$ and $\mathbf{B}^{\mathbf{prox}}$ are polynomials of order $l_p \in \mathbf{Z}_{>0}$ and $l_e \in \mathbf{Z}_{>0}$, respectively, and $\omega \in \mathbf{R}_{>0}$ and $\gamma \in \mathbf{R}_{>0}$ are weights associated to each term. Using these higher order matrices, triUMPF applies two NMFs to recover communities (Appx. Section B.2 [21]). Then, triUMPF uses $\mathbf{W}$ and $\mathbf{H}$ from the decomposition phases (Sect. 2.1) and the detected communities to optimize multi-label pathway parameters in an iterative process (Appx. Section B.3 [21]) until the maximum number of allowed iterations is reached. At the end, the trained model can be used to perform pathway prediction from a newly annotated genome or multi-organismal dataset with high precision due to constraints embedded in the P2E, P2P, and E2E associations matrices.

3 Experiments

We evaluated triUMPF performance across multiple datasets spanning the genomic information hierarchy [20]: i) - T1 golden consisting of EcoCyc, Human-Cyc, AraCyc, YeastCyc, LeishCyc, and TrypanoCyc; ii) - three *E. coli* genomes composed of E. coli K-12 substr. MG1655 (TAX-511145), uropathogenic E. coli str. CFT073 (TAX-199310), and enterohemorrhagic E. coli O157:H7 str. EDL933

Table 1. Average precision of each comparing algorithm on 6 golden T1 data.

Methods	Average precision score					
	EcoCyc	HumanCyc	AraCyc	YeastCyc	LeishCyc	TrypanoCyc
PathoLogic	0.7230	**0.6695**	0.7011	0.7194	**0.4803**	**0.5480**
MinPath	0.3490	0.3004	0.3806	0.2675	0.1758	0.2129
mlLGPR	0.6187	0.6686	0.7372	0.6480	0.4731	0.5455
triUMPF	**0.8662**	0.6080	**0.7377**	**0.7273**	0.4161	0.4561

(TAX-155864); iii) - BioCyc (v20.5 T2 & 3) [5] composed of 9255 PGDBs (Pathway/Genome Databases) constructed using Pathway Tools v21 [14]; iv) - *symbionts* genomes of *Moranella* (GenBank NC-015735) and *Tremblaya* (GenBank NC-015736) encoding distributed metabolic pathways for amino acid biosynthesis [22]; v)- Critical Assessment of Metagenome Interpretation (CAMI) initiative low complexity dataset consisting of 40 genomes [27]; and vi) - whole genome shotgun sequences from the Hawaii Ocean Time Series (HOTS) at 25 m, 75 m, 110 m (sunlit) and 500 m (dark) ocean depth intervals [29]. General statistics about these datasets are summarized in Appx. Table 4 [21]. For comparative analysis, triUMPF's performance on T1 golden datasets was compared to three pathway prediction methods: i) - MinPath version 1.2 [33], which uses integer programming to recover a conserved set of pathways from a list of enzymatic reactions; ii) - PathoLogic version 21 [14], which is a symbolic approach that uses a set of manually curated rules to predict pathways; and iii) - mlLGPR which uses supervised multi-label classification and rich feature information to predict pathways from a list of enzymatic reactions [20]. In addition to testing on T1 golden datasets, triUMPF performance was compared to PathoLogic on three *E. coli* genomes and to PathoLogic and mlLGPR on mealybug symbionts, CAMI low complexity, and HOTS multi-organismal datasets. The following metrics were used to report on performance of pathway prediction algorithms including: *average precision, average recall, average F1 score (F1)*, and *Hamming loss* as described in [20]. For experimental settings and additional tests, see Appx. Sections D and E [21].

3.1   T1 Golden Data

As shown in Table 1, triUMPF achieved competitive performance against the other methods in terms of average precision with optimal performance on Eco-Cyc (0.8662). However, with respect to average F1 scores, it under-performed on HumanCyc and AraCyc, yielding average F1 scores of 0.4703 and 0.4775, respectively (Appx. Table 5 [21]). Since triUMPF was trained using BioCyc containing less than 1460 trainable pathways in comparison to the remaining pathway prediction methods, it is expected to produce a sizable set of accurate pathways from organismal genomes.

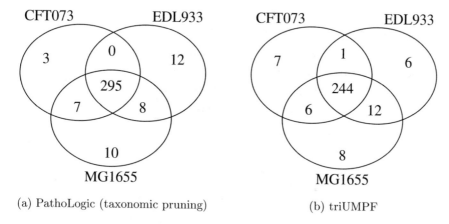

(a) PathoLogic (taxonomic pruning)   (b) triUMPF

Fig. 2. A three way set difference analysis of pathways predicted for E. coli K-12 substr. MG1655 (TAX-511145), E. coli str. CFT073 (TAX-199310), and E. coli O157:H7 str. EDL933 (TAX-155864) using (a) PathoLogic (taxonomic pruning) and (b) triUMPF.

3.2   Three E. coli Data

Recall that community detection (Sect. 2.2) was used to guide the multi-label learning process. To demonstrate the influence of communities on pathway prediction, we compared pathways predicted for the T1 gold standard E. coli K-12 substr. MG1655 (TAX-511145), henceforth referred to as MG1655, using Patho-Logic and triUMPF. Appx. Fig. 8a [21] shows the results, where both methods inferred 202 true-positive pathways (green-colored) in common out of 307 expected true-positive pathways (using EcoCyc as a common frame of reference). In addition, PathoLogic uniquely predicted 39 (magenta-colored) true-positive pathways while triUMPF uniquely predicted 16 true-positives (purple-colored). This difference arises from the use of taxonomic pruning in PathoLogic which improves recovery of taxonomically constrained pathways and limits false-positive identification. With taxonomic pruning enabled, PathoLogic inferred 79 false-positive pathways, and over 170 when pruning was disabled. In contrast triUMPF which does not use taxonomic feature information inferred 84 false-positive pathways (Appx. Table 6 [21]). This improvement over PathoLogic with pruning disabled reinforces the idea that pathway communities improve precision of pathway prediction with limited impact on overall recall. Based on these results, it is conceivable to train triUMPF on subsets of organismal genomes resulting in more constrained pathway communities for pangenome analysis.

To further evaluate triUMPF performance on closely related organismal genomes, we performed pathway prediction on E. coli str. CFT073 (TAX-199310), and E. coli O157:H7 str. EDL933 (TAX-155864) and compared results to the MG1655 reference strain [31]. Both CFT073 and EDL933 are pathogens infecting the human urinary and gastrointestinal tracts, respectively. Previously, Welch and colleagues described extensive genomic mosaicism between these strains and MG1655, defining a core backbone of conserved metabolic genes

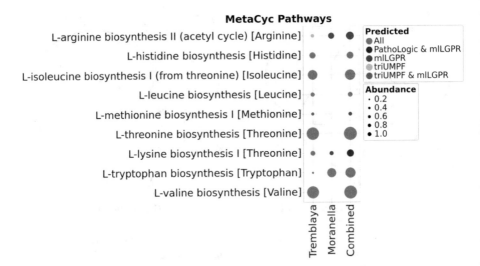

Fig. 3. Comparative study of predicted pathways for symbiotic data between Patho-Logic, mlLGPR, and triUMPF. The size of circles corresponds the associated coverage information.

interspersed with genomic islands encoding common pathogenic or niche defining traits [31]. Neither CFT073 nor EDL933 genomes are represented in the BioCyc collection of organismal pathway genome databases. A total of 335 and 319 unique pathways were predicted by PathoLogic and triUMPF, respectively. The resulting pathway lists were used to perform a set-difference analysis with MG1655 (Fig. 2). Both methods predicted more than 200 pathways encoded by all three strains including core pathways like the *TCA* cycle (Appx. Figs. 8b and 8c [21]). CFT073 and EDL933 were predicted to share a single common pathway (*TCA cycle IV (2-oxoglutarate decarboxylase)*) by triUMPF. However this pathway variant has not been previously identified in E. coli and is likely a false-positive prediction based on recognized taxonomic range. Both PathoLogic and triUMPF predicted the *aerobactin biosynthesis* pathway involved in siderophore production in CFT073 consistent with previous observations [31]. Similarly, four pathways (e.g. *L-isoleucine biosynthesis III* and *GDP-D-perosamine biosynthesis*) unique to EDL933 were inferred by both methods.

Given the lack of cross validation standards for CFT073 and EDL933 we were unable to determine which method inferred fewer false-positives across the complete set of predicted pathways. To constrain this problem on a subset of the data, we applied GapMind [25] to analyze amino acid biosynthesis pathways encoded in MG1655, CFT073 and EDL933 genomes. GapMind is a web-based application developed for annotating amino acid biosynthesis pathways in prokaryotic microorganisms (bacteria and archaea), where each reconstructed pathway is supported by a confidence level. After excluding pathways that were not incorporated in the training set, a total of 102 pathways were identified across the three strains encompassing 18 amino acid biosynthesis pathways and 27 path-

Table 2. Predictive performance of mlLGPR and triUMPF on CAMI low complexity data. For each performance metric, '↓' indicates the smaller score is better while '↑' indicates the higher score is better.

Metric	mlLGPR	triUMPF
Hamming loss (↓)	0.0975	**0.0436**
Average precision score (↑)	0.3570	**0.7027**
Average recall score (↑)	**0.7827**	0.5101
Average F1 score (↑)	0.4866	**0.5864**

way variants with high confidence (Appx. Table 7 [21]). PathoLogic inferred 49 pathways identified across the three strains encompassing 15 amino acid biosynthesis pathways and 17 pathway variants while triUMPF inferred 54 pathways identified across the three strains encompassing 16 amino acid biosynthesis pathways and 19 pathway variants including *L-methionine biosynthesis* in MG1655, CFT073 and EDL933 that was not predicted by PathoLogic. Neither method was able to predict *L-tyrosine biosynthesis I* (Appx. Fig. 10 [21]).

3.3   Mealybug Symbionts Data

To evaluate triUMPF performance on distributed metabolic pathways, we used the reduced genomes of *Moranella* and *Tremblaya* [22]. Collectively the two symbiont genomes encode intact biosynthesis pathways for 9 essential amino acids. PathoLogic, mlLGPR, and triUMPF were used to predict pathways on individual symbiont genomes and a composite genome consisting of both, and resulting amino acid biosynthesis pathway distributions were determined (Fig. 3). Both triUMPF and PathoLogic predicted 6 of the expected amino acid biosynthesis pathways on the composite genome while mlLGPR predicted 8 pathways. The pathway for phenylalanine biosynthesis (*L-phenylalanine biosynthesis I*) was excluded from analysis because the associated genes were reported to be missing during the ORF prediction process. False positives were predicted for individual symbiont genomes in *Moranella* and *Tremblaya* using both methods although pathway coverage was reduced in relation to the composite genome.

3.4   CAMI and HOTS Data

To evaluate triUMPF's performance on more complex multi-organismal genomes, we used the CAMI low complexity [27] and HOTS datasets [29] comparing resulting pathway predictions to both PathoLogic and mlLGPR. For CAMI low complexity, triUMPF achieved an average F1 score of 0.5864 in comparison to 0.4866 for mlLGPR which is trained with more than 2500 labeled pathways (Table 2). Similar results were obtained for HOTS (see Appx. Section E.4 [21]). Among a subset of 180 selected water column pathways, PathoLogic and triUMPF predicted a total of 54 and 58 pathways, respectively, while mlL-GPR inferred 62. From a real world perspective none of the methods predicted pathways for *photosynthesis light reaction* nor *pyruvate fermentation to (S)-acetoin* although both are expected to be prevalent in the water column. Perhaps, the absence of specific ECs associated with these pathway limits rule-based or ML prediction. Indeed, closer inspection revealed that the enzyme *catabolic acetolactate synthase* was missing from the *pyruvate fermentation to (S)-acetoin* pathway, which is an essential rule encoded in PathoLogic and represented as a feature in mlLGPR. Conversely, although this pathway was indexed to a community, triUMPF did not predict its presence, constituting a false-negative.

4   Conclusion

In this paper we introduced a novel ML approach for metabolic pathway inference that combines three stages of NMF to capture relationships between enzymes and pathways within a network followed by community detection to extract higher order network structure. First, a Pathway-EC association (**M**) matrix, obtained from MetaCyc, is decomposed using the NMF technique to learn a constrained form of the pathway and EC factors, capturing the microscopic structure of **M**. Then, we obtain the community structure (or mesoscopic structure) jointly from both the input datasets and two interaction matrices, Pathway-Pathway interaction and EC-EC interaction. Finally, the consensus relationships between the community structure and data, and between the learned factors from **M** and the pathway labels coefficients are exploited to efficiently optimize metabolic pathway parameters. We evaluated triUMPF performance using a corpora of experimental datasets manifesting diverse multi-label properties comparing pathway prediction outcomes to other prediction methods including PathoLogic [14] and mlLGPR [20]. During benchmarking we realized that the BioCyc collection suffers from a class imbalance problem [11] where some pathways infrequently occur across PGDBs. This results in a significant sensitivity loss on T1 golden data, where triUMPF tended to predict more frequently observed pathways while missing more infrequent pathways. One potential approach to solve this class-imbalance problem is subsampling the most informative PGDBs for training, hence, reducing false-positives [16]. Despite the observed class imbalance problem, triUMPF improved pathway prediction precision without the need for taxonomic rules or EC features to constrain metabolic potential. From an ML perspective this is a promising outcome considering that triUMPF was trained on a reduced number of pathways relative to mlLGPR. Future development efforts will explore subsampling approaches to improve sensitivity and the use of constrained taxonomic groups for pangenome and multi-organismal genome pathway inference.

References

1. Bairoch, A.: The ENZYME database in 2000. Nucleic Acids Res. **28**(1), 304–305 (2000)
2. Bro, R., Smilde, A.K.: Principal component analysis. Anal. Methods **6**(9), 2812–2831 (2014)
3. Carbonell, P., et al.: Selenzyme: enzyme selection tool for pathway design. Bioinformatics **34**(12), 2153–2154 (2018)
4. Caspi, R., et al.: The MetaCyc database of metabolic pathways and enzymes and the BioCyc collection of pathway/genome databases. Nucleic Acids Res. **44**(D1), D471–D480 (2016)
5. Caspi, R., et al.: BioCyc: online resource for genome and metabolic pathway analysis. FASEB J. **30**(1 Supplement), lb192 (2016)
6. Dale, J.M., Popescu, L., Karp, P.D.: Machine learning methods for metabolic pathway prediction. BMC Bioinform. **11**(1), 1 (2010)
7. Fortunato, S., Hric, D.: Community detection in networks: a user guide. Phys. Rep. **659**, 1–44 (2016)
8. Fu, X., Huang, K., Sidiropoulos, N.D., Ma, W.K.: Nonnegative matrix factorization for signal and data analytics: identifiability, algorithms, and applications. arXiv preprint arXiv:1803.01257 (2018)
9. Hahn, A.S., Konwar, K.M., Louca, S., Hanson, N.W., Hallam, S.J.: The information science of microbial ecology. Curr. Opin. Microbiol. **31**, 209–216 (2016)
10. Hanson, N.W., Konwar, K.M., Hawley, A.K., Altman, T., Karp, P.D., Hallam, S.J.: Metabolic pathways for the whole community. BMC Genomics **15**(1) (2014). Article number: 619. https://doi.org/10.1186/1471-2164-15-619
11. He, H., Garcia, E.A.: Learning from imbalanced data. IEEE Trans. Knowl. Data Eng. **21**(9), 1263–1284 (2009)
12. Jiao, D., Ye, Y., Tang, H.: Probabilistic inference of biochemical reactions in microbial communities from metagenomic sequences. PLoS Comput. Biol. **9**(3), e1002981 (2013)
13. Kanehisa, M., Furumichi, M., Tanabe, M., Sato, Y., Morishima, K.: KEGG: new perspectives on genomes, pathways, diseases and drugs. Nucleic Acids Res. **45**(D1), D353–D361 (2017)
14. Karp, P.D., et al.: Pathway tools version 19.0 update: software for pathway/genome informatics and systems biology. Brief. Bioinform. **17**(5), 877–890 (2016)
15. Konwar, K.M., Hanson, N.W., Pagé, A.P., Hallam, S.J.: MetaPathways: a modular pipeline for constructing pathway/genome databases from environmental sequence information. BMC Bioinform. **14**(1) (2013). Article number: 202. https://doi.org/10.1186/1471-2105-14-202
16. Lakshminarayanan, B., Pritzel, A., Blundell, C.: Simple and scalable predictive uncertainty estimation using deep ensembles. In: Advances in Neural Information Processing Systems, pp. 6402–6413 (2017)
17. Lawson, C.E., et al.: Common principles and best practices for engineering microbiomes. Nat. Rev. Microbiol. **17**(12), 725–741 (2019)
18. Li, Y., Wang, Y., Zhang, T., Zhang, J., Chang, Y.: Learning network embedding with community structural information. In: Proceedings of the Twenty-Eighth International Joint Conference on Artificial Intelligence, IJCAI-2019, pp. 2937–2943. International Joint Conferences on Artificial Intelligence Organization, July 2019

19. M. A. Basher, A.R., Hallam, S.J.: Leveraging heterogeneous network embedding for metabolic pathway prediction. Bioinformatics (2020). https://doi.org/10.1093/bioinformatics/btaa906
20. M. A. Basher, A.R., McLaughlin, R.J., Hallam, S.J.: Metabolic pathway inference using multi-label classification with rich pathway features. PLoS Comput. Biol. **16**(10), 1–22 (2020)
21. M. A. Basher, A.R., McLaughlin, R.J., Hallam, S.J.: Metabolic pathway inference using non-negative matrix factorization with community detection. BioRxiv (2020). https://doi.org/10.1101/2020.05.27.119826
22. McCutcheon, J.P., Von Dohlen, C.D.: An interdependent metabolic patchwork in the nested symbiosis of mealybugs. Curr. Biol. **21**(16), 1366–1372 (2011)
23. McDonald, A.G., Boyce, S., Tipton, K.F.: ExplorEnz: the primary source of the IUBMB enzyme list. Nucleic Acids Res. **37**(suppl 1), D593–D597 (2009)
24. Natarajan, N., Dhillon, I.S.: Inductive matrix completion for predicting gene-disease associations. Bioinformatics **30**(12), i60–i68 (2014)
25. Price, M.N., et al.: Filling gaps in bacterial amino acid biosynthesis pathways with high-throughput genetics. PLoS Genet. **14**(1), e1008106 (2018)
26. Rossi, R.A., Jin, D., Kim, S., Ahmed, N.K., Koutra, D., Lee, J.B.: From community to role-based graph embeddings. arXiv preprint arXiv:1908.08572 (2019)
27. Sczyrba, A., et al.: Critical assessment of metagenome interpretation–a benchmark of metagenomics software. Nat. Methods **14**(11), 1063 (2017)
28. Shafiei, M., Dunn, K.A., Chipman, H., Gu, H., Bielawski, J.P.: BiomeNet: a Bayesian model for inference of metabolic divergence among microbial communities. PLoS Comput. Biol. **10**(11), e1003918 (2014)
29. Stewart, F.J., Sharma, A.K., Bryant, J.A., Eppley, J.M., DeLong, E.F.: Community transcriptomics reveals universal patterns of protein sequence conservation in natural microbial communities. Genome Biol. **12**(3), R26 (2011)
30. Toubiana, D., et al.: Combined network analysis and machine learning allows the prediction of metabolic pathways from tomato metabolomics data. Commun. Biol. **2**(1), 1–13 (2019). Article number: 214
31. Welch, R.A., et al.: Extensive mosaic structure revealed by the complete genome sequence of uropathogenic Escherichia coli. Proc. Natl. Acad. Sci. **99**(26), 17020–17024 (2002)
32. Yang, Z., Michailidis, G.: A non-negative matrix factorization method for detecting modules in heterogeneous omics multi-modal data. Bioinformatics **32**(1), 1–8 (2015)
33. Ye, Y., Doak, T.G.: A parsimony approach to biological pathway reconstruction/inference for genomes and metagenomes. PLoS Comput. Biol. **5**(8), e1000465 (2009)

A Novel Pathway Network Analytics Method Based on Graph Theory

Subrata Saha[1] , Ahmed Soliman[2] , and Sanguthevar Rajasekaran[2(✉)]

[1] Columbia University Irving Medical Center, New York, NY 10032, USA
ss6265@cumc.columbia.edu
[2] Department of Computer Science and Engineering, University of Connecticut,
Storrs, CT 06269, USA
{ahmed.soliman,sanguthevar.rajasekaran}@uconn.edu

Abstract. A biological pathway is an ordered set of interactions between intracellular molecules having collective activity that impacts cellular function, for example, by controlling metabolite synthesis or by regulating the expression of sets of genes. They play a key role in advanced studies of genomics. However, existing pathway analytics methods are inadequate to extract meaningful biological structure underneath the network of pathways. They also lack automation. Given these circumstances, we have come up with a novel graph theoretic method to analyze disease-related genes through weighted network of biological pathways. The method automatically extracts biological structures, such as clusters of pathways and their relevance, significance of each pathway and gene, and so forth hidden in the complex network. We have demonstrated the effectiveness of the proposed method on a set of genes associated with coronavirus disease.

Keywords: Biological pathway · Coronavirus disease 2019 (COVID-19) · Weighted network · Gene ontology · Disease ontology

1 Introduction

Identifying the functional correlations among molecular components is very crucial to accurately deciphering the structure-function interdependencies. Usually, most of the biological activities are not stemming from a single molecule but a set of molecules interacting in a concerted way (for instance, polygenic disorders). Consequently, deciphering biology under the context of networks is very crucial and promising. From the perspective of graph theory, a biological network consists of a set of nodes representing specific biological entities. Two nodes are connected by an edge depicting an affiliation between them. Based on the characteristic of a network, an edge can be directed or undirected. The weight of an edge defines similarity or dissimilarity between the two participating nodes, such as semantic similarity, Pearson's coefficient, etc. For instance, in protein–protein interaction (PPI) networks, nodes and edges represent proteins and physical

© Springer Nature Switzerland AG 2021
S. K. Jha et al. (Eds.): ICCABS 2020, LNBI 12686, pp. 45–55, 2021.
https://doi.org/10.1007/978-3-030-79290-9_5

interactions, respectively [20,23]. For another instance, in metabolic networks, nodes serve as metabolites and edges are links for these metabolites engaging in the same biochemical reactions [11,15]. In this context, accurately identifying functional modules (i.e. clusters) in biological network is very critical because it helps us to figure out the underneath structure, interactions, and dynamics of cell functions [8,21].

Applying biological network analytics to a set of genes related to a specific disease has been done before by several researchers. For example, Hu et al. have taken a pathway-based approach and applied a network analysis method to understand the molecular features of Alzheimer's disease [14]. Other researchers have proposed mining algorithms targeting protein-protein interaction networks (PPINs) for Homo sapiens. Theses algorithms are designed to discover functional modules (clusters) of protein complexes. This is because such densely connected sub-graphs usually lead to substantial biological knowledge at the molecular level. As an example, Sriwastava et al. have proposed a quasi-clique mining method for detecting these dense regions [22]. Melo et al. have used a Machine Learning approach to detect such hot spots [17]. In their work they used 27 algorithms with different cost functions and reported the best algorithm.

In this article, we have proposed a novel methodology for analyzing complex network of biological pathways. It is scale-free, i.e. there is no hard thresholding to discard edges based on weight. It runs in 4 stages. At first, it picks a set of enriched biological pathways for a given set of disease-related genes. Later, it constructs a weighted network where each pathway acts as a node. Two nodes are connected by an edge if they have some common biological entities and the weight of this edge refers to that similarity. Here, our similarity score is well defined and its values are ranging from 0 to 1. At the third stage, it clusters the network into a set of non-overlapping groups having highest modularity. Finally, it ranks the pathways based on their significance.

The rest of the paper is organized as follows. Our proposed methodology is described in Sect. 2. Results and some relevant discussions are portrayed in Sect. 3 and Sect. 4 concludes the paper.

2   Methods

Our proposed algorithm consists of 4 basic steps as stated earlier. At the beginning, we find a set of statistically significant biological pathways with respect to a curated list of disease-related genes. We then form a network of pathways by employing an innovative weighted network construction method. At the third step, we detect a set of sub-networks by clustering the entire network. Finally, we analyze each of the sub-networks based on *closeness centrality*. Pseudocode of our proposed method can be found in Algorithm 1. Next, we illustrate our proposed method in detail.

Algorithm 1. Pathway Network Analytics Method

Input: A set of disease-related genes G, shared genes s, and common genes c.
Output: A set of functional modules, pathway influences.

1: Let D be a database of biological pathways (such as Reactome, KEGG, etc.);
2: Pick a set of pathways $P_{interim} \in D$ with respect to G where each pathway $p \in P$ contains at least c number of common genes in G;
3: Retain statistically significant pathways $P \in P_{interim}$ by employing hypergeometric overrepresentation test;
4: Initialize a weighted network N where each pathway $p \in P$ acts as a node;
5: **for** each distinct and ordered pair $(p_i, p_j) \in P$ **do**
6:      $t_i \leftarrow p_i \cap G$
7:      $t_j \leftarrow p_j \cap G$
8:      **if** $|t_i \cap t_j| \geq s$ **then**
9:          Compute the similarity score $l_{p_i p_j}$ between p_i and p_j using Equation 1;
10:          **if** $l_{p_i p_j} > 0$ **then**
11:              Add an edge $e_{p_i p_j}$ in network N;
12:              Weight of edge $e_{p_i p_j}$, $w_{p_i p_j} \leftarrow l_{p_i p_j}$;
13:          **end if**
14:      **end if**
15: **end for**
16: Calculate the influence score of each pathway $p \in P$ using *closeness centrality*;
17: Cluster the network N by a suitable graph clustering algorithm;
18: **for** each cluster $q \in Q$ **do**
19:      Calculate the influence score of each pathway $p \in q$ using *closeness centrality*;
20: **end for**
21: Return the clusters, influence scores, etc.

2.1   Identification of Significantly Enriched Pathways

At first, we find a set of biological pathways from the database of pathways (e.g. Reactome, KEGG, etc.) with respect to a given set of disease-related genes (i.e. a set of genes known to be responsible for a specific disease, such as Alzheimer's, Parkinson's, or COVID-19). Later, we employ hypergeometric test that uses the hypergeometric distribution (https://en.wikipedia.org/wiki/Hypergeometric_distribution) to calculate the statistical significance of a biological pathway with respect to the given set of genes. Specifically, we computed a hypergeometric p-value for each of the biological pathways to assess whether a pathway is over-represented with those genes. Finally, we choose a set of enriched pathways having Bonferroni corrected p-value < 0.05.

2.2   Construction of a Weighted Network

We build an undirected weighted graph to investigate interlinks and interactions among the enriched biological pathways. Let $G(V, E, w)$ be our undirected weighted graph where each enriched pathway $v \in V$ acts as a vertex. Two vertices v_i and v_j will be connected by an edge $e \in E$ iff (1) v_i and v_j share at least x common genes and (2) the similarity between v_i and v_j is $>$ a threshold, t. In our experiment, x and t were set to 2 and 0, respectively (i.e. there is no hard thresholding). We define similarity between any two vertices in a way so that it mimics a specific biological theme between them, if any. The similarity between any two genes can roughly be defined by their common gene ontology (GO) terms. The "biological process" sub-ontology of GO (GO-BP) is widely used to evaluate sets of relationships between genes. It is due to the fact that genes annotated with the same (or related) GO-BP terms are functionally homogeneous. Consequently, two pathways will be functionally similar if they contain a set of functionally related genes between them. By considering this observation, we compute the pair-wise Jaccard index between any two pathways. Suppose, v_i and v_j pathways consist of G_i and G_j sets of genes of size m and n, respectively. Let's assume, $G_i = \{g_1^i, g_2^i, \ldots, g_m^i\}$ and $G_j = \{g_1^j, g_2^j, \ldots, g_n^j\}$. We then extract the number of common GO-BP terms and divide it by the total number of unique terms of each pair of genes g^i and g^j possess to get the Jaccard index. We add all such indices and normalize the final value by dividing it by the number of such pairs to get the similarity score. As a result, the minimum and maximum value of such a score will be 0 and 1, respectively. Intuitively, the higher the score, the more will be two pathways functionally similar. Now, the score constitutes the weight of the edge between v_i and v_j. Assume, g_p^i and g_q^j ($1 \le p \le m$ and $1 \le q \le n$, respectively) contain the sets of b_p^i and b_q^j GO-BP terms, respectively. The similarity score between any two vertices can then be mathematically formulated as:

$$S(v_i, v_j) = \frac{\sum_m \sum_n \frac{|b_m^i \cap b_n^j|}{|b_m^i \cup b_n^j|}}{m \times n} \tag{1}$$

2.3   Identification of Sub-networks

Clustering is one of the most widely used techniques for exploratory data analysis. The goal here is to divide the biological pathways into several groups such that each group of pathways represents a specific and distinct biological event/theme. As the network of biological pathways often constitutes a small number of nodes (≤ 50), we employed an optimal community structure prediction algorithm [7]. It calculates the optimal community structure of a graph, by maximizing the modularity measure over all possible partitions. Please, note that modularity optimization is an NP-complete problem. Consequently, all known algorithms have exponential time complexity in worst case. So, it is impossible to run exact algorithms on a graph with large number of nodes having dense connections. Louvain method is an attractive alternative in this context [6]. The method is a greedy optimization method having time complexity $\mathcal{O}(n \cdot log^2 n)$ where n is the number of nodes in the network.

2.4   Identification of Important Pathways

In graph theory and network analysis, *centrality* is a very crucial notion in identifying influential nodes in a graph. It is used to measure the importance of distinct nodes in a graph. Applications include but are not limited to identifying the most influential person(s) in a social network, key infrastructure nodes in the Internet or urban networks, super-spreaders of disease, and so forth. Depending on the definition of *centrality*, it comes in contrasting essences. Simplest one is the *degree centrality*, which is defined as the number of edges incident on a particular node. A natural extension of *degree centrality* is *closeness centrality*. In a connected graph, *closeness centrality* of a node is a measure of *centrality* in a network, calculated as the reciprocal of the sum of the length of the shortest paths between the node and all other nodes in the graph [4]. Consequently, the more "central" a node is, the more closer it is to all other nodes in the graph. Mathematically it is defined as: $C(x) = \frac{1}{\sum_y d(y,x)}$ where $d(y,x)$ is the distance between node x and node y. We have used *closeness centrality* as a metric to identify influential pathways both in the entire network and corresponding subnetworks. We normalize the score by multiplying it by $n-1$ where n is the total number of nodes in the network. It is to be noted that we have replaced the weight of each edge with $1 - weight$ before computing the *closeness centrality*.

3   Results and Discussions

3.1   Dataset Employed

To demonstrate the effectiveness of our proposed methodology, we have performed rigorous experimental evaluations by considering a set of human protein-coding genes linked to SARS-CoV-2 infection and COVID-19 disease. These genes are curated from GENCODE (https://www.gencodegenes.org/human/covid19.html). The list of genes consists of 560 genes extrapolated from recent publications and in collaboration with other projects, such as recently published drug repurposing studies by Zhou et al. [26] and Gordon et al. [12]. Throughout the article, we dubbed this set of genes as covid-genes.

3.2   Outcomes and Relevant Discussions

As stated in Sect. 2, our network analytics method runs in 4 stages. Next, we illustrate the experimental evaluations based on those stages in details.

3.2.1   Pathway Enrichment Analysis

At first, we chose a set of enriched biological pathways from database of pathways. In this study, Reactome [10] pathways were utilized to decipher the biological theme from the set of 560 covid-genes. Here is a brief review of Reactome database. Reaction is the "nucleus" of the Reactome data model. A set of entities, such as nucleic acids, proteins, complexes, and small molecules engages in reactions to form a network of biological interactions and are ultimately assembled into pathways. Some notable examples of biological pathways in Reactome database consist of signaling, innate and acquired immune function, transcriptional regulation, translation, apoptosis, and classical intermediary metabolism.

After employing hypergeometric test, we detect 30 Bonferroni corrected (adjusted $p < 0.05$) biological pathways. Table 1 contains these 30 significant pathways. It is to be noted that we only retain those enriched pathways each having at least 5 genes in common with covid-genes to discard potentially spurious and smaller pathways. Next we discuss about some of the enriched pathways. At first, consider interferon signaling pathways. Interferons, also known as type I, type II, and type III interferons in humans, are proteins produced by cells in response to infection. Insufficient or inappropriately timed activation of interferon signaling may contribute to severe cases of COVID-19 caused by the coronavirus SARS-CoV-2 [5,13,19]. Now, consider basigin interactions pathway. Basigin (BSG, in short) also known as extracellular matrix metallo-proteinase inducer (EMMPRIN) or cluster of differentiation 147 (CD147) is a protein encoding gene [16]. According to Wang et al. [25] host-cell-expressed basigin (CD147) may bind spike protein of SARS-CoV-2 and possibly be involved in host cell invasion.

Table 1. Bonferroni corrected enriched Reactome pathways. G_p refers to the number of genes a pathway contains. G_c refers to the common genes between a pathway and covid-genes.

Pathway	Reactome ID	p-value	G_p	G_c
Interferon alpha/beta signaling	R-HSA-909733	5.93E−12	70	22
Interferon Signaling	R-HSA-913531	4.57E−09	158	29
Influenza Infection	R-HSA-168254	2.06E−08	63	17
Basigin interactions	R-HSA-210991	3.63E−08	26	11
MHC class II antigen presentation	R-HSA-2132295	4.98E−08	59	16
Disease	R-HSA-1643685	9.80E−07	508	54
Metabolism of Angiotensinogen to Angiotensins	R-HSA-2022377	1.05E−06	17	8
Interactions of Rev with host cellular proteins	R-HSA-177243	2.33E−06	37	11
Peptide hormone metabolism	R-HSA-2980736	3.14E−06	53	13
Influenza Life Cycle	R-HSA-168255	3.14E−06	53	13
Host Interactions of HIV factors	R-HSA-162909	4.17E−06	89	17
Mitochondrial protein import	R-HSA-1268020	6.85E−06	65	14
Nuclear import of Rev protein	R-HSA-180746	7.54E−06	34	10
Transport of Ribonucleoproteins into the Host Nucleus	R-HSA-168271	1.82E−05	30	9
NEP/NS2 Interacts with the Cellular Export Machinery	R-HSA-168333	1.82E−05	30	9
ISG15 antiviral mechanism	R-HSA-1169408	1.82E−05	30	9
Export of Viral Ribonucleoproteins from Nucleus	R-HSA-168274	2.44E−05	31	9
Activation of Matrix Metalloproteinases	R-HSA-1592389	2.44E−05	31	9
Metabolism of proteins	R-HSA-392499	2.59E−05	2000	146
Trafficking and processing of endosomal TLR	R-HSA-1679131	2.91E−05	13	6
TRAF3-dependent IRF activation pathway	R-HSA-918233	2.91E−05	13	6
Rev-mediated nuclear export of HIV RNA	R-HSA-165054	4.24E−05	33	9
Nuclear Pore Complex (NPC) Disassembly	R-HSA-3301854	5.49E−05	34	9
Neutrophil degranulation	R-HSA-6798695	5.66E−05	485	47
Cellular response to heat stress	R-HSA-3371556	6.93E−05	99	16
SUMOylation of DNA replication proteins	R-HSA-4615885	1.13E−04	37	9
Regulation of Glucokinase by GRP	R-HSA-170822	1.35E−04	30	8
Degradation of the extracellular matrix	R-HSA-1474228	1.42E−04	105	16
Negative regulators of DDX58/IFIH1 signaling	R-HSA-936440	1.44E−04	23	7
TRAF6 mediated IRF7 activation	R-HSA-933541	1.75E−04	17	6

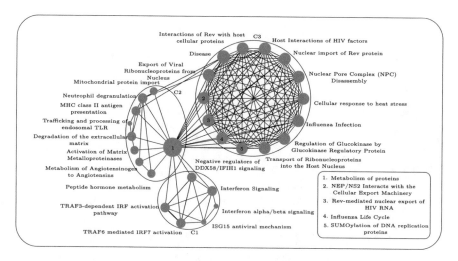

Fig. 1. Entire network built from 30 statistically significant pathways.

3.2.2 Entire Network Analysis

After finding the statistically significant pathways, we build a network as stated in Sect. 2. We found 243 covid-genes (out of 560) in the enriched 30 Reactome pathways. Enrichment analyses based on GO-BP and DO terms have been performed with respect to those 243 covid-genes.

GO-BP Enrichment Analysis. One of the main uses of the GO terms is to perform enrichment analysis on a given set of genes. For instance, an enrichment analysis will find which GO terms are over-represented (or under-represented) using annotations for that set of genes. We have performed enrichment analysis on 243 covid-genes based on GO-BP terms and retained 163 GO-BP Bonferroni corrected (adjusted $p < 0.05$) terms. Top 10 enriched GO-BP terms can be found in Table 2. Most of the terms are associated with COVID-19 disease.

Table 2. Bonferroni corrected top 10 enriched GO-BP terms.

ID	Description	Gene ratio	p-value	Adjusted p
GO:0019058	viral life cycle	39/243	3.61E−28	1.35E−24
GO:0043312	neutrophil degranulation	47/243	2.17E−27	8.14E−24
GO:0002283	neutrophil activation involved in immune response	47/243	2.85E−27	1.07E−23
GO:0042119	neutrophil activation	47/243	6.97E−27	2.61E−23
GO:0002446	neutrophil mediated immunity	47/243	7.62E−27	2.85E−23
GO:0043903	regulation of symbiosis encompassing mutualism through parasitism	32/243	2.23E−25	8.34E−22
GO:1903900	regulation of viral life cycle	28/243	2.66E−25	9.98E−22
GO:0050792	regulation of viral process	30/243	8.35E−25	3.13E−21
GO:0051607	defense response to virus	32/243	9.31E−24	3.49E−20
GO:0009615	response to virus	35/243	1.88E−22	7.04E−19

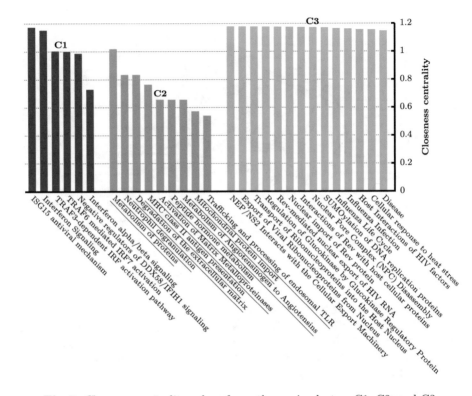

Fig. 2. *Closeness centrality* values for pathways in clusters C1, C2, and C3.

DO Enrichment Analysis. Like GO, the disease ontology (DO) is a formal ontology of human disease. We have performed enrichment analysis on the set of top 243 covid-genes as noted above based on DO terms and retained 7 DO Bonferroni corrected (adjusted $p < 0.05$) terms (please, see Table 3). Almost all of the retained enriched DO terms are associated with COVID-19 disease. For instance, Wafa et al. [3] reported the first case of hepatitis B virus (HBV) reactivation caused by COVID-19 in a young adult with altered mental status and severe transaminitis.

Table 3. Bonferroni corrected enriched DO terms.

ID	Description	Gene ratio	p-value	Adjusted p-value
DOID:2237	hepatitis	31/150	5.23E−11	2.93E−08
DOID:8469	influenza	16/150	2.4E−10	1.35E−07
DOID:2043	hepatitis B	19/150	3.72E−09	2.08E−06
DOID:3459	breast carcinoma	20/150	2.81E−05	0.0157
DOID:1883	hepatitis C	15/150	2.86E−05	0.016
DOID:184	bone cancer	15/150	4.66E−05	0.0261
DOID:3347	osteosarcoma	14/150	4.72E−05	0.0264

Pathway Significance. As noted earlier, after constructing the network, we compute the influence of each pathway based on *closeness centrality*. The corresponding network is shown in Fig. 1. The influence of each pathway with respect to the entire network is proportional to the diameter of its representative circle. "Metabolism of proteins" and "Trafficking and processing of endosomal TLR" pathways posses the highest (0.91) and lowest (0.36) *centrality* scores, respectively.

Table 4. Top 6 most occurring covid-genes in each cluster. N_P refers to the number of pathways a specific gene is found. $\%O$ represents the fraction of such pathways.

C1			C2			C3		
Gene	N_P	$\%O$	Gene	N_P	$\%O$	Gene	N_P	$\%O$
IRF3	6	100	CTSG	6	67	RAE1	14	100
DDX58	5	83	CTSD	5	56	NUP88	14	100
TRIM25	5	83	MME	4	44	NUP58	14	100
IRF7	4	67	CTSB	4	44	NUP98	14	100
ISG15	4	67	CTSK	4	44	NUP54	14	100
MX1	3	50	CTSS	4	44	NUP210	14	100

3.2.3   Sub-network Analysis

After constructing the weighted network, we cluster the network to find functional modules. Since the weight of an edge corresponds to the functional similarity between two pathways, please see Sect. 2, each of the sub-networks consisting of highly interconnected pathways should mimic a specific biological theme or functionality. Please note that our network is scale-free, i.e. there is no thresholding on weights. Also we do not need to provide the number of clusters *a priori*. The clustering algorithm automatically dismantles the entire weighted network into 3 groups, namely C1, C2, and C3. Figure 1 shows the entire network along with cluster annotations. We have also computed pathway *centrality* scores for each of the sub-networks as shown in Fig. 2.

At first, consider C1 cluster. It consists of 6 pathways and all of them are related to immune systems in humans. Therefore, our proposed method accurately classify a set of interrelated and analogous pathways into a group. According to the *centrality* measure "ISG15 antiviral mechanism" is the most influential pathway in this cluster. It is a potential regulator of the immune response from viral infection. As reported by [24] viral de-ISGylases, including SARS-CoV-2 PL^{pro}, positively modulate ISG15 secretion. Now, please, see Table 4 for the top 6 most occurring covid-genes in cluster C1. IRF3 appears in all the 6 pathways. It plays a critical role in the innate immune system's response to viral infection [9].

C2 sub-network contains 9 pathways and is very interesting. It is a mix of protein metabolism and immune system related pathways. Several studies (such as [18]) demonstrated the strong link between immune cell function and protein metabolism. Table 4 contains top 6 most occurring covid-genes in cluster

C2. CTSG has been found in 6 (out of 9) pathways. According to [2], it was significantly altered in naso-oropharyngeal samples of SARS-CoV-2 patients.

Finally, C3 consists of 14 pathways. Almost all of them are related to some specific viral infections. Please, see Table 4 for the top 6 most occurring covidgenes in cluster C3. All the top genes have been found in all the 14 pathways. As reported by [1], SARS-CoV-2 ORF6 disrupts nucleocytoplasmic transport through interactions with RAE1 and NUP98.

4 Conclusions

In this article, we have proposed a formal framework to decipher complex structure among the interacting biological pathways. To begin with, a set of enriched biological pathways are identified with respect to a set of disease-related genes. An innovative weighted network is then constructed. It is scale-free, i.e. there is no hard thresholding to discard edges based on weights. The weighted network is then disassembled to find a set of non-overlapping and functionally different clusters. We have demonstrated its effectiveness by employing a set of genes potentially associated with the COVID-19 disease.

References

1. Addetia, A., et al.: SARS-CoV-2 ORF6 disrupts nucleocytoplasmic transport through interactions with Rae1 and Nup98. BioRxiv (2020)
2. Akgun, E., et al.: Altered molecular pathways observed in naso-oropharyngeal samples of SARS-CoV-2 patients. medRxiv (2020)
3. Aldhaleei, W.A., Alnuaimi, A., Bhagavathula, A.S.: COVID-19 induced hepatitis B virus reactivation: a novel case from the United Arab Emirates. Cureus **12**(6), e8645 (2020)
4. Bavelas, A.: Communication patterns in task-oriented groups. J. Acoust. Soc. Am. **22**(6), 725–730 (1950)
5. Blanco-Melo, D., et al.: Imbalanced host response to SARS-CoV-2 drives development of COVID-19. Cell **181**(5), 1036–1045 (2020)
6. Blondel, V.D., Guillaume, J.L., Lambiotte, R., Lefebvre, E.: Fast unfolding of communities in large networks. J. Stat. Mech: Theory Exp. **2008**(10), P10008 (2008)
7. Brandes, U., et al.: On modularity clustering. IEEE Trans. Knowl. Data Eng. **20**(2), 172–188 (2007)
8. Bu, D., et al.: Topological structure analysis of the protein-protein interaction network in budding yeast. Nucleic Acids Res. **31**(9), 2443–2450 (2003)
9. Collins, S.E., Noyce, R.S., Mossman, K.L.: Innate cellular response to virus particle entry requires IRF3 but not virus replication. J. Virol. **78**(4), 1706–1717 (2004)
10. Croft, D., et al.: Reactome: a database of reactions, pathways and biological processes. Nucleic Acids Res. **39**(suppl_1), D691–D697 (2010)
11. Duarte, N.C., et al.: Global reconstruction of the human metabolic network based on genomic and bibliomic data. Proc. Natl. Acad. Sci. **104**(6), 1777–1782 (2007)
12. Gordon, D., Jang, M.G., Bouhaddou, M., Krogan, N.J.: A SARS-CoV-2-human protein-protein interaction map reveals drug targets and potential drug-repurposing (2020)

13. Hadjadj, J., et al.: Impaired type I interferon activity and exacerbated inflammatory responses in severe COVID-19 patients. medRxiv (2020). https://doi.org/10. 1101/2020.04.19.20068015. https://www.medrxiv.org/content/early/2020/04/23/ 2020.04.19.20068015

14. Hu, Y.S., Xin, J., Hu, Y., Zhang, L., Wang, J.: Analyzing the genes related to Alzheimer's disease via a network and pathway-based approach. Alzheimer's Res. Ther. **9**(1), 1–15 (2017). https://doi.org/10.1186/s13195-017-0252-z

15. Jeong, H., Tombor, B., Albert, R., Oltvai, Z.N., Barabási, A.L.: The large-scale organization of metabolic networks. Nature **407**(6804), 651–654 (2000)

16. Kasinrerk, W., Fiebiger, E., Stefanova, I., Baumruker, T., Knapp, W., Stockinger, H.: Human leukocyte activation antigen M6, a member of the Ig superfamily, is the species homologue of rat OX-47, mouse basigin, and chicken HT7 molecule. J. Immunol. **149**(3), 847–854 (1992)

17. Melo, R., et al.: A machine learning approach for hot-spot detection at protein-protein interfaces. Int. J. Mol. Sci. **17**(8), 1215 (2016)

18. Odegaard, J.I., Chawla, A.: The immune system as a sensor of the metabolic state. Immunity **38**(4), 644–654 (2013). https://doi.org/10.1016/j.immuni.2013.04.001

19. Park, A., Iwasaki, A.: Type I and type III interferons-induction, signaling, evasion, and application to combat COVID-19. Cell Host Microbe **27**(6), 870–878 (2020)

20. Rual, J.F., et al.: Towards a proteome-scale map of the human protein-protein interaction network. Nature **437**(7062), 1173–1178 (2005)

21. Spirin, V., Mirny, L.A.: Protein complexes and functional modules in molecular networks. Proc. Natl. Acad. Sci. **100**(21), 12123–12128 (2003)

22. Sriwastava, B.K., Basu, S., Maulik, U.: A quasi-clique mining algorithm for analysis of the human protein-protein interaction network. In: Shankar, B.U., Ghosh, K., Mandal, D.P., Ray, S.S., Zhang, D., Pal, S.K. (eds.) PReMI 2017. LNCS, vol. 10597, pp. 411–417. Springer, Cham (2017). https://doi.org/10.1007/978-3-319-69900-4_52

23. Stelzl, U., et al.: A human protein-protein interaction network: a resource for annotating the proteome. Cell **122**(6), 957–968 (2005)

24. Swaim, C.D., Canadeo, L.A., Monte, K.J., Khanna, S., Lenschow, D.J., Huibregtse, J.M.: Modulation of extracellular ISG15 signaling by pathogens and viral effector proteins. Cell Rep. **31**(11), 107772 (2020)

25. Wang, K., et al.: SARS-CoV-2 invades host cells via a novel route: CD147-spike protein. BioRxiv (2020)

26. Zhou, Y., Hou, Y., Shen, J., Huang, Y., Martin, W., Cheng, F.: Network-based drug repurposing for novel coronavirus 2019-nCoV/SARS-CoV-2. Cell Discov. **6**(1), 1–18 (2020)

Latent Variable Modelling and Variational Inference for scRNA-seq Differential Expression Analysis

Joana Godinho[1,2], Alexandra M. Carvalho[1], and Susana Vinga[2,3(✉)]

[1] Instituto de Telecomunicações, Instituto Superior Técnico, ULisboa, Lisbon, Portugal
[2] INESC-ID, Instituto Superior Técnico, ULisboa, Lisbon, Portugal
[3] IDMEC, Instituto Superior Técnico, ULisboa, Lisbon, Portugal
susanavinga@tecnico.ulisboa.pt

Abstract. Disease profiling, treatment development, and the identification of new cell populations are some of the most relevant applications relying on differentially expressed genes (DEG) analysis. Three leading technologies emerged; namely, DNA microarrays, bulk RNA sequencing (RNA-seq), and single-cell RNA sequencing (scRNA-seq), the main focus of this work. We introduce two novel approaches to assess DEG: extended Bayesian zero-inflated negative binomial factorization (ext-ZINBayes) and single-cell differential analysis (SIENA). We benchmark the proposed methods with known DEG analysis tools using two real public datasets. The results show that the two procedures can be very competitive with existing methods (scVI, SCDE, MAST, and DEseq) in identifying relevant putative biomarkers. In terms of scalability and correctness, SIENA stands out and may emerge as a powerful tool to discover functional differences between two conditions. Both methods are publicly available at https://github.com/JoanaGodinho/.

Keywords: scRNA-seq · Latent variable models · Variational inference

1 Introduction

Gene expression is a biological process that affects how living organisms operate. Studying and understanding gene expression leads to a broader knowledge of how cells work and how they evolve. With this knowledge, groundbreaking advances can be achieved in the fields of genetics, molecular biology, and medicine.

One of the most relevant tasks performed through gene expression assessment is the identification of differentially expressed genes (DEG). DEG are genes that show different expression levels across different types of cells. With DEG

Supported by FCT PTDC/CCI-CIF/29877/2017, DSAIPA/DS/0026/2019, PTDC/CCI-BIO/4180/-2020, UIDB/50008/2020, UIDB/50021/2020, UIDB/50022/2020 and EU H2020 951970.

© Springer Nature Switzerland AG 2021
S. K. Jha et al. (Eds.): ICCABS 2020, LNBI 12686, pp. 56–68, 2021.
https://doi.org/10.1007/978-3-030-79290-9_6

identification, we can deepen our understanding on cell differentiation, study disease phenotypes, and assess how certain treatments perform [12].

Research has provided several computational methods aiming to carry out such task. Initially, differential expression (DE) analysis was only performed using gene expression obtained from DNA microarrays. Then, technological advances empowered the emergence of RNA sequencing (RNA-seq) protocols to profile gene expression. In a first approach, DE analysis over bulk RNA data was performed using packages, such as Limma [15], that were initially designed to account for microarray input. However, due to differences between microarray and RNA-seq data, new methods, such as DEseq [1] and edgeR [14], were developed specifically for the latter.

In more recent years, single-cell RNA sequencing (scRNA-seq) has stood out from the previous two. The appeal for this kind of data is the possibility to perform detailed analysis with high-resolution data, given that gene expression is described by mRNA counts in individual cells. Nonetheless, the data is still subject to the presence of noise, which unfolds as extra variation and false zero counts, caused by dropout events, batch effects, stochastic gene expression, or variations in sequencing depth (or library size). In order to prevent wrong conclusions, one must seek to disentangle correct biological information from the noisy data. One suitable approach is to use a latent variable model (LVM). Methods such as SCDE [10], MAST [7], and scVI [11] take this approach to identify DEG. However, there is a need for new techniques, since scRNA-seq datasets are becoming increasingly larger, making some of the existent methods inefficient.

In this work, we propose two new methods to perform DE analysis (DEA): ext-ZINBayes (extended Bayesian zero-inflated negative binomial) and SIENA (SIngle-cEll differeNtial Analysis). Both rely on a LVM and variational inference (VI). ext-ZINBayes adopts ZINBayes [6], developed for dimensionality reduction. SIENA operates under a new LVM defined based on existing models. We benchmark their performances with other methods, using two public datasets.

2   Methods

To build a scRNA-seq analysis method, one must account for the presence of confounding factors. Using a LVM has shown to be a reliable approach to separate the additional variability added by such factors. In a latent variable model, variables are either observed or unobserved (latent). The latent variables (Z) are responsible for capturing and describing hidden factors that influence the observed variables (X). So, in the single-cell RNA context, the observed variables would be the counts, and the latent would describe the confounding factors.

The main idea behind VI [3] is to find a tractable distribution $q(Z)$ that best approximates the posterior. To do so, it assumes that $q(Z)$ belongs to a family of distributions, defined by parameters v. From a more in-depth perspective, VI aims to find the parameter values that make $q(Z)$ closest to $p(Z|X)$. To evaluate the dissimilarity between the distributions, VI relies on the Kullback-Leibler (KL) divergence, calculated as $\mathbb{E}_{q(Z)}[\log q(Z) - \log p(Z|X)]$, where $\mathbb{E}_{q(Z)}$ is the expected value with respect to $q(Z)$. Finding the optimal v amounts to finding v which minimize th previous equation. However, the KL divergence involves the unknown posterior, thus an alternative metric is required. This metric is known as the Evidence Lower BOund (ELBO) and is derived from the KL divergence. The ELBO is calculated as $\mathbb{E}_{q(Z)}[\log p(Z, X) - \log q(Z)]$. In this case, to find v, one maximizes the ELBO. The performance of VI techniques is greatly influenced by the choice of the family Q [3]. The most commonly used is the mean-field variational family, which assumes independence between all latent variables. As such, each unobserved variable follows a separate variational distribution. Then, for a set of N latent variables, $q(Z)$ can be obtained through $q(Z) = \prod_{j=1}^{N} q(Z_j)$.

2.1   ext-ZINBayes

This method is an extension of ZINBayes [6], developed for dimensionality reduction. With an additional feature, we enable it to detect DEG. ZINBayes aimed to create an approach able to discover a true biological representation of the data, without the distortion caused by noise factors, taking into consideration batch effects, dropout events, and stochastic gene expression. The model is built upon a Gamma-Poisson mixture so each count follows a Negative Binomial (NB) distribution, to account for overdispersion of RNA-seq data. However, it may not be sufficient to account for the excessive amount of zeros caused by dropout events. Therefore, zero-inflation (ZI) was added to the generative process.

For a given set of G genes and N cells, the count of each gene g in cell i is defined by X_{ig}, where $1 \leq g \leq G$ and $1 \leq i \leq N$. X_{ig} is either governed by the NB component or, in case of a dropout, is modelled as a constant zero. Thus,

$$D_{ig} \sim \text{Bernoulli}(\pi_{ig}) \qquad\qquad Y_{ig} \sim \text{Poisson}(\lambda_{ig})$$

$$\lambda_{ig} \sim \text{Gamma}\left(\theta_g, \frac{\theta_g}{\rho_{ig}L_i}\right) \qquad\qquad X_{ig} = \begin{cases} Y_{ig} & \text{if } D_{ig} = 0 \\ 0 & \text{otherwise} \end{cases},$$

where Y_{ig} generates the count's magnitude if D_{ig} indicates that X_{ig} is not a dropout. λ_{ig} parameterizes Y_{ig} corresponding to the mean expression of g in i. L_i is a scale factor linked to the library size of cell i, i.e., the total amount of transcripts detected in cell i, while θ_g corresponds to a dispersion factor related to gene g. Both are seen as latent random variables, $L_i \sim \text{Lognormal}(\mu_i, \sigma_i)$ and $\theta_g \sim \text{Gamma}(2, 1)$. The formulations ρ_{ig} and π_{ig} correspond, respectively, to the percentage of transcripts of gene g in cell i and the probability of X_{ig} being a dropout. These yield both cell-specific and gene-specific features: $C_i = [Z_i, s_i]$, $\rho_{ig} = \frac{C_i W_{0,g}}{\sum_g C_i W_{0,g}}$, and $\text{logit}(\pi_{ig}) = C_i W_{1,g}$. The cell-related features are the batch and the K-dimensional biological signature of the cell (s_i and Z_i). The gene-related are the factor loadings $W_{0,g}$ and $W_{1,g}$. While s_i is a B-sized one-hot representation, with B being the number of batches, Z_i, $W_{0,g}$, and $W_{1,g}$ are collections of random variables whose components are modelled as follows: $W_{0,gk'} \sim \text{Gamma}(0.1, 0.3)$, $W_{1,gk'} \sim \text{Normal}(0, 1)$ and $Z_{ik} \sim \text{Gamma}(2, 1)$, where $0 \leq k \leq K$ and $0 \leq k' \leq K + B$ [6]. Given the model's definition, exact inference can not be performed due to the intractability of the posteriors. The model is not conditionally conjugate, making it impossible to use coordinate ascent VI (CAVI). Thus, reparameterization gradients (RG) was used.

To identify DEG between two cell subpopulations, we adopted the procedure developed in [11]. For each gene g, we define two hypotheses given a pair of cells from different populations. Both cells are from the same batch and have counts x_1 and x_2: $H_a^g = \rho_{1g} > \rho_{2g}$ and $H_b^g = \rho_{1g} \leq \rho_{2g}$. The first hypothesis states that the percentage of transcripts of gene g in cell 1 is higher than in cell 2, while the second hypothesis translates into the opposite. Then, a Bayes factor, B, is calculated as: $B = \frac{p(H_a^g|x_1,x_2)\ p(H_a^g)}{p(H_b^g|x_1,x_2)\ p(H_b^g)}$. Its value quantifies the ratio between the likelihood probabilities given each hypothesis. High factors reflect stronger beliefs over H_a^g, while factors closer to zero reflect more support over H_b^g. To simplify the assessment of the probability ratio, we consider the factor's logarithm and not its raw value. If the logarithm is negative, it means H_b^g is more prone to be true; if it is positive, it means the opposite: H_a^g is more likely correct. This implies that higher positive values yield higher supports over H_a^g, whereas lower negative values yield higher supports over the alternative hypothesis. Given that H_a^g and H_b^g are mutually exclusive and have equal prior probabilities, i.e., $p(H_a^g) = p(H_b^g)$, $\log(B)$ is calculated as: $\log(B) = \log \frac{p(H_a^g|x_1,x_2)}{1-p(H_a^g|x_1,x_2)} = \log(p(H_a^g|x_1,x_2)) - \log(1 - p(H_a^g|x_1,x_2))$. To compute the posterior $p(H_a^g|x_1,x_2)$, the probabilities ρ_{1g} and ρ_{2g}, which make H_a^g true, need to be summed. Given that the ρ values depend on Z_1, Z_2, and $W_{0,g}$, we need to integrate all possible combinations of the three that yield H_a^g true,

$$p(H_a^g|x_1, x_2) = \iiint_{(w_{0,g}, z_1, z_2)} \mathbb{I}[\rho_{1g} > \rho_{2g}]\ q(z_1)\ q(z_2)\ q(w_{0,g}). \tag{1}$$

In the equation above, $q(z_1)$ and $q(z_2)$ correspond to the probabilities of cell 1 having a z_1 representation and cell 2 having a z_2 representation, $q(w_{0,g})$ corresponds to the probability of gene g having $w_{0,g}$ has its loading factors. Each of these probabilities is obtained through the corresponding variational distribution shaped during inference.

Since calculating the exact value of the integral is very computationally demanding, we used Monte-Carlo approximation. Thus, $p(H_a^g|x_1,x_2)$ is an empirical average of $\rho_{1g} > \rho_{2g}$ over a random set of triplets $(z_1, z_2, w_{0,g})$ sampled from the variational distributions, where $|S|$ is the total number of samples assessed:

$$p(H_a^g|x_1, x_2) \approx \frac{1}{|S|} \sum_{(w_{0,g}, z_1, z_2)} \mathbb{I}[\rho_{1g} > \rho_{2g}]. \tag{2}$$

This process is performed over all possible cell pairs that contain one cell from each of the two subpopulations under study. However, the ρ values are affected by s, which is responsible for specifying the batches. Thus, the process is only viable if all cells come from the same batch. When the counts come from two or more batches, each cell must be paired with another cell from the same batch but with different types/populations. If inter-batch pairs were allowed, the differences between the cells' ρ could be biased by batch effects. The factor's logarithm of each pair is then averaged and the resulting mean used as a score. Above a threshold value between 2 and 3 (see [9]), the gene is classified as a DEG. To scale this procedure to very large datasets, the method enables the use of a subset of cell pairs. If the dataset contains cells from only one batch, we simply randomly pick the specified number of pairs. On the other hand, if the dataset gathers multiple batches, the proportion of pairs from each batch in the subset is equal to the proportion of each batch in the original dataset.

2.2 SIENA

For our second proposed method, we designed a new LVM, where each count follows a zero-inflated NB (ZINB) distribution. As we mentioned before, with a ZINB distribution, one can depict the overdispersion and the excess of zero entries, typical of scRNA data. Like in ZINBayes, the NB is built through a Gamma-Poisson mixture.

We decided to adopt several variables used both in ZINBayes and in scVI, making our model able to account for noise factors such as different library sizes, dropouts, and stochastic gene expression. The major difference is the removal of indicators s and variables Z, which specify the batches and the low dimensional representations of each cell's biological features. Below we present the model, where X_{ig} reports the number of reads mapped to gene g in cell i:

$$L_i \sim \text{Lognormal}\,(\mu_i, \sigma_i) \qquad \beta_{ig} \sim \text{Gamma}\left(\frac{1}{3}, 1\right) \qquad \rho_{ig} = \frac{\beta_{ig}}{\sum_g \beta_{ig}}$$

$$\lambda_{ig} \sim \text{Gamma}\,(\theta_g L_i \rho_{ig}, \theta_g) \qquad Y_{ig} \sim \text{Poisson}\,(\lambda_{ig}) \qquad D_{ig} \sim \text{Bernoulli}\,(\pi_{ig})$$

$$X_{ig} = \begin{cases} Y_{ig} & \text{if } D_{ig} = 0 \\ 0 & \text{otherwise} \end{cases}.$$

On one hand, variables L_i, ρ_{ig}, D_{ig}, and λ_{ig} encode the same as in ZINBayes. L_i is a scaling factor, ρ_{ig} is the percentage of gene g transcripts in cell i, λ_{ig} is the expression mean, and D_{ig} indicates if count X_{ig} is a dropout. On the other hand, θ_g, the gene's dispersion factor, is not seen as a random variable, but as a non-random model parameter, and π_{ig}, the probability of a dropout event, is defined as a hyperparameter. Nonetheless, these are not the only differences between this model and ZINBayes's.

Similarly to [11], L_i is drawn from a log-normal where the mean and variance of the underlying normal, μ_i and σ_i, are set, respectively, as the mean and the variance of the log scaled sequencing depths/library sizes considering only cells from the same batch as cell i. In ZINBayes, μ_i and σ_i are the mean and variance of the log library sizes considering all cells. The choice to model L_i as a log-normal is to restrict its domain to be positive since it's a scaling factor. Note that L_i encodes a factor proportionally related to the sequencing depth; it is not the actual sequencing depth, as pointed out in [11]. As an alternative, we also tested L_i as a Gamma, where its mean and variance are equal to the mean and variance of the library sizes in i's batch.

Regarding ρ_{ig}, they are set as the ratio between a factor related to gene g and cell i, β_{ig}, and the sum of cell i factors with each gene. We take this formulation to not only restrict $\rho \in [0, 1]$ but also $\sum_g \rho_{ig} = 1$. Both of these conditions need to be imposed because ρ_{ig} reflects a percentage, which translates into a relative frequency. An alternative approach would be to model ρ as a Beta distribution. However, using a Beta does not fit ρ properly since it only complies with the domain constraint. Moreover, given that no biological representation is defined for each cell, the biological variability is implicitly described by variable ρ. Notwithstanding, each ρ may be affected by the cell's batch since no batch-specific variable is modelled.

For the latent factors β_{ig}, we chose to posit a Gamma with $\alpha = \frac{1}{3}$ and $\beta = 1$ because it leads to a distribution where most of its probability density is placed near zero, yet its expected value is $\frac{1}{3}$. Due do its tail, this Gamma generates, in each cell, very low factors for most genes, but higher factors for a restricted set. In theory, this set is composed by cell i highly expressed genes.

As mentioned before, the NB is attained through a Gamma-Poisson mixture determined by variables λ_{ig} and Y_{ig}, according to the following:

$$\text{If } X \sim \text{Poisson}\,(\lambda) \text{ and } \lambda \sim \text{Gamma}\,(r, \frac{1-p}{p}) \text{ then } X \sim \text{NB}\,(r, p). \quad (3)$$

In this formulation, the NB output is defined as the number of successes until r failures occur, given a p probability of success. As a result, its expected value is $\frac{rp}{1-p}$. This is the NB formulation taken in our model. When deciding the parameters of λ_{ig}'s Gamma, we aimed to fix the NB expected value as $L_i\rho_{ig}$. By defining the shape as $\theta_g L_i\rho_{ig}$ and rate as θ_g we achieve that.

Finally, zero-inflation is employed by variable D_{ig}, which determines if X_{ig} is necessarily zero. D_{ig} is drawn from a Bernoulli distribution, since D_{ig} only needs to take two values, one indicating dropout occurrence and another one stating non-occurrence. The probability of the Bernoulli, π_{ig}, is set as the proportion of zero entries of gene g over all cells from the same type and batch as cell i. For instance, if 60% of gene g counts in type A and batch 1 cells are zero, then π_{ig} is set as 0.6 for all type A and batch 1 cells.

Regarding inference, we use reparameterization gradients. We resort to VI because the counts' marginal likelihood is intractable, so exact inference can not be applied. In addition, the model is not conditionally conjugate, so CAVI can not be implemented. However, to use RG, variable D_{ig} needs to be discarded since it is not differentiable. As such, instead of defining X_{ig} with a conditional assignment, we set it as a mixture of two components: one is the NB while the other models the zero-inflation, generating only zeros. The ZI part is determined by a Deterministic distribution, which takes only the value zero, so all its density is placed over that value. Given that in a ZI model, zeros can be generated from the two components, the likelihood of X_{ig} is calculated as follows: $p(X_{ig}|\beta_i, L_i) = \pi_{ig} \times p_{\text{Det}}(X_{ig}) + (1 - \pi_{ig}) \times p_{\text{NB}}(X_{ig}|\beta_i, L_i)$. As we can see from the equation above, we manage to also integrate out λ_{ig} and Y_{ig}, due to Eq. (3). As such, the RG mechanism merely has to find a distribution q, which approximates $p(\beta_i, L_i | X_i)$. The variational distribution $q(\beta_i, L_i)$ is considered mean-field, and thus can be factorized in $q(\beta_i)$ and $q(L_i)$; $q(\beta_i)$ can be further factorized into $\prod_{i=1}^{G} q(\beta_{ig})$. Both $q(L_i)$ and $q(\beta_{ig})$ distributions are assumed to be log-normal since β_{ig} and L_i are positive variables, and RG performs better when it has to optimize normal distributions.

We build two inference networks: one outputs $q(\beta_i)$ parameters, i.e., the mean and variance of each of its $q(\beta_{ig})$; the other generates the mean and variance for $q(L_i)$. With this approach, we are able to scale inference to very large datasets, since optimization is carried only over global variables, the weights, instead of local variables, the means and variances. Each network has one hidden layer with 128 nodes, and its output layer has two heads, one for the mean(s) and another one for the variance(s). A sotfplus transformation is applied over the variance head, to restrict it to be positive. In the hidden layer, a batch normalization step is employed before activation. In addition to the neural networks, memory-wise scalability is improved via batch training where, in each iteration, we break the full dataset into several subsets with equal size and use each one to do an update step. Regarding θ_g optimization, we iteratively set it as a Maximum Likelihood Estimation (MLE), after one update step over the networks' weights. Therefore, after inference, θ_g will have a value that maximizes the likelihood of the counts given the obtained optimal variational parameters.

To assess if a given gene g is a DEG, we apply the same procedure as in ext-ZINBayes. Given a cell pair, we define two exclusive hypotheses like the ones in Sec. 2.1. Then, log scaled Bayes factors are calculated for each cell pair, and the absolute value of their average is used as a metric to classify g as DEG/non-DEG. The difference from the ext-ZINBayes procedure is the calculation of $p(H_a^g | x_1, x_2)$; in this approach, ρ_{ig} only depends on β_i. Consequently, it is only necessary to integrate all combinations of β_1 and β_2 that make H_a^g true:

$$p(H_a^g | x_1, x_2) = \iint\limits_{(\beta_1, \beta_2)} \mathbb{I}[\rho_{1g} > \rho_{2g}] \, q(\beta_1) \, q(\beta_2). \tag{4}$$

This integral is also approximated through Monte Carlo, where the samples are drawn from β_1 and β_2 variational distributions. Given that, in our model, we do not specify any variable identifying each cell's batch, the ρ values will be tampered by batch effects. To overcome this, we only pair cells that come from the same batch, just like in ext-ZINBayes. This way, the DE analysis is more truthful to biological differences. Furthermore, we scale the Bayes factor calculation by providing the optional use of a subset of pairs.

3   Results

To assess the performance of ZINBayes and SIENA, we used two known real scRNA-seq datasets: Islam and PBMC (Peripheral Blood Mononuclear Cells).

Since none of the datasets has the genes identified as being DEG or not, we considered as ground truth the ones detected in the corresponding microarray dataset using Limma, similarly to [4,10].

The Islam dataset [8] contains expression counts of 92 embryonic cells of the house mouse: 48 Embryonic stem (ES) cells and 44 Embryonic fibroblast (MEF) cells. The PBMC is a droplet-based dataset that contains count data of human peripheral blood mononuclear cells, which were sequenced in two different batches. The cells are divided into four different types, where 4996 are CD4+ T cells, 1448 are CD8+ T cells, 1621 are B cells, and 339 are Dendritic cells, which amount to a total of 8404 cells. Regarding the gold standard results, we used the microarray dataset Moliner [13] for the comparison between ES and MEF cells and two microarray datasets of PBMC, one for the CD4+T vs. CD8+T analysis and the other for the B vs. Dendritic analysis. To obtain the Islam and the two PBMC microarray datasets (CD4+T vs. CD8+T and B vs. Dendritic), we used the GEO database [5] using the codes GSE29087, GSE8835, and GSE29618, respectively. The single-cell PBMC dataset is a subset of the one used in [11]. For Moliner, we extracted the data from the .CEL files used in [4].

As a preprocessing step, we filtered out the genes in the single-cell datasets that were not in the corresponding microarray datasets and vice-versa. In addition, genes for which there was no information about their length were also removed, since MAST implements a TPM (Transcripts per Million) normalization, that requires the length. As such, DE analysis between types ES and MEF was carried out over 6757 genes, while for the CD4+T vs. CD8+T and B vs. Dendritic analyses, only 3346 genes were evaluated.

We first assess the effects of different settings of SIENA, and ext-ZINBayes, then we benchmark their performances with existing methods: SCDE, MAST, scVI, and DEseq. The first three were designed specifically for scRNA data, whereas DEseq is used for both bulk and single-cell data. To run MAST and DEseq, we used the corresponding R packages available on the Bioconductor project. For SCDE, we used the R implementation provided by the authors, and for scVI, we used the Python release 0.3.0. Finally, we compare the biological conclusions drawn from each methods' rank through a gene set enrichment analysis (GSEA), where we compare the Gene Ontology (GO) [2].

Inspired by what the authors in [16] concluded, we decided to evaluate how the zero-inflation affected SIENA and ext-ZINBayes. The full analysis is available in a Supplementary File (https://github.com/JoanaGodinho/).

To compare our methods' and the four mentioned DE procedures', we used as a benchmark measure the average AUC. Out of the four, only MAST and DEseq are deterministic. The results are shown in Fig. 1. To generate the bar plot, we ran and calculated the AUC of MAST and DEseq only one time, whereas, for the other methods, we repeated the process 50 times and averaged the AUC values. Both scVI and SIENA were run with gene dispersion and without ZI. Ext-ZINBayes was also operated without ZI, but unlike for SIENA and scVI, no dispersion was adopted. With Islam each run had 1000 epochs (for the three methods), while with PBMC, each run of SIENA and scVI had 500 epochs.

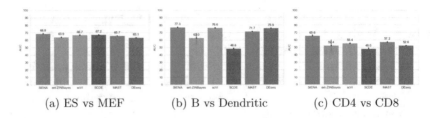

(a) ES vs MEF (b) B vs Dendritic (c) CD4 vs CD8

Fig. 1. Average AUC values for each method with the Islam dataset and PBMC.

As seen in Fig. 1a, with the Islam dataset, SIENA yields better results show-ing an average AUC close to 69%, while DEseq has the lowest average out of all the methods. Nonetheless, SIENA presents a higher variation (5%), given that two runs generated an AUC~64%. All the differences between the average AUC are statistically significant (Welch's t-tests, p-values < 0.01). Regarding Fig. 1b analysis, all methods, except SCDE and ext-ZINBayes, present a higher average AUC when conducting DE analysis between B and Dendritic cells than between ES and MEF. SCDE is the only that shows a great decrease in performance, having an average AUC $< 50\%$, whereas SIENA stands out as the best with an average AUC of 77.3%. Unlike in the ES vs. MEF test, ext-ZINBayes shows the highest variance. Regarding the CD8 vs. CD4 comparison (Fig. 1c), SIENA obtains the best mean AUC (65%), while all the other methods perform con-siderably worst, having an average AUC $< 60\%$. Once again, SCDE shows the worst AUC. Like in the B vs. Dendritic test, ext-ZINBayes shows the highest variance in the results. For both SIENA and ext-ZINBayes, the log Bayes factors were calculated using a subset of cell pairs. More specifically, 7.5×10^5 pairs were used, and, for each of those pairs, 100 samples of ρ were computed.

In both PBMC tests, obtained AUC are more divergent than the ones gath-ered in ES vs. MEF test. While in the latter, the difference between the average AUC of the best method and the worst is slightly lower than 6%, in B vs. Den-dritic and CD4 vs. CD8 tests, the difference is around 30% and 20%, respectively. Almost all mean AUC differences are statistically significant for both PBMC comparisons (Welch's t-tests, p-values < 0.01), expect ext-ZINBayes and DEseq in the CD4 vs. CD8 test (p-value $= 0.075$).

Besides AUC calculations, it is also pivotal to assess how each method scores the genes, i.e., how certain they are that a given gene is a DEG. We compare for each gene in the Islam dataset, the DE metrics of each method with the p-values obtained by Limma. The full results are available in the Supplementary File.

Given the poor results under the CD4 vs. CD8 test, we deepen our analysis over the test with an intersection graph in Fig. 2, without considering the results from Limma. To generate the plot, we considered the 50 runs of SIENA, SCDE, scVI, and ext-ZINBayes conducted for the AUC analysis, and for each method, we calculated the median DE score of each gene. Then, we gathered the top 1000 genes with the highest medians. For MAST and DEseq, we gathered the top 1000 genes with the lowest FDR adjusted p-values of only one run.

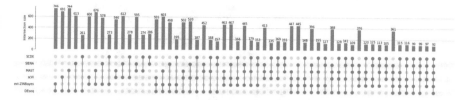

Fig. 2. Intersections of the top 1000 DEG (CD4 vs. CD8 analysis). Matrix dots specify method combinations; bars encode the number of DEG in common.

We can see that ext-ZINBayes and DEseq have almost 750 in common, which was expected given that the two methods have essentially the same average AUC. In fact, the pair has the largest intersection set out of all duos. DEseq has also more genes in common with SIENA than any other method. This is curious given that MAST and scVI show average AUC closer to SIENA's. Furthermore, all two method combinations considering SCDE have the lowest number of genes in common, when compared with the other two methods combinations. The same happens for three, four, and five method combinations. Moreover, if we consider all methods except SCDE, the number of genes in common goes from 92 to 361; it increases almost four times, whereas if one of the other methods is not considered, it only increases to values between 97 and 116. The only method that comes close to identify the same DEG as SCDE is SIENA, yet the number of genes in common is just a bit over 25%.

After gathering a DE ranking, the next step in any DE analysis is to perform enrichment analysis to extract biological meaning. As such, it is important to compare the biological features outlined by each method's list. To do so, we used the STRING [17] platform to compare the gene ontologies enriched by the top DEG of each method under the B vs. Dendritic analysis. For SIENA, ext-ZINBayes, scVI, and SCDE, we calculated the median DE score of each gene over the 50 runs considered in Fig. 1b. Then, we used the medians to rank the genes in descending order. For MAST and DEseq, we used the rank of one run.

For the ground truth (Limma's) rank, 18 GO terms were considered significantly enriched, i.e., had an enrichment FDR corrected p-value ≤ 0.01. SIENA's rank led to 73 terms, ext-ZINBayes to 62, DEseq to 56, MAST to 41, and scVI to 31. Figure 3 illustrates for each method, the enrichment score of a set of GO terms. From the heatmap, we can see that the top 10 GO terms for SIENA and ext-ZINBayes are the same as for the ground truth list. However, the scores related to ext-ZINBayes are greatly higher. Even though DEseq has one different term, it has a closer score signature to the ground truth than ext-ZINBayes. Out of all methods, scVI shows the most divergent GO pattern. Notwithstanding, all methods seem to detect DEG connected to biological terms like myeloid leukocyte activation and leukocyte/myeloid cell activation involved in immune response, meaning that differences between B and Dendritic cells are probably related with such processes.

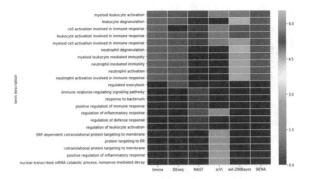

Fig. 3. GO enrichment analysis for each method (B vs. Dendritic test). Each term is one of the 10 most significantly enriched terms of at least one method.

In both SIENA and ext-ZINBayes, configurations without zero-inflation lead to better results in the two real datasets, in contrast with what research has assumed throughout the years. Nonetheless, as we stated before, the authors in [16] disproved this assumption for droplet-based data, thus supporting our findings regarding the PBMC dataset. Even though the authors affirm that in the case of plate-based counts zero-inflation mechanisms are necessary, our results with the Islam counts may refute such conclusions, since that dataset has probably a plate-based origin due to its small number of cells (< 100).

Comparing to existing methods, SIENA was able to detect more accurately the DEG in both PBMC and Islam analysis. In addition, SIENA exhibited the most consistent behaviour over the three real data tests, showing average AUC ranging from 65% to 78%. All the other methods presented more fluctuating performances when dealing with different types of datasets. This means that SIENA is more adequate to deal with both small and large datasets than some state-of-the-art methods. Moreover, SIENA is able to scale its memory usage during both inference and DE test computation without decreasing its overall accuracy, a crucial feature given the exponential growth of data size.

Of the two proposed methods, SIENA shows overall rankings more correlated with the ground truth rankings. Moreover, in pair with DEseq, SIENA leads to biological conclusions closer to the ones drawn from the ground truth. Taking all this into account, we can conclude that only SIENA is able to compete with state-of-the-art procedures, managing to assemble more truthful DE scores in a more feasible amount of time.

4   Conclusion

We proposed two new Bayesian probabilistic procedures to assess DE. Both are built upon LVMs and DE mechanisms. Ext-ZINBayes adopts an existing probabilistic model designed for dimensionality reduction. It performs DE analysis using some of the model's latent variables. SIENA devises a novel model, leveraging certain assumptions taken in state-of-the-art methods. Of the two procedures, SIENA yields the best results, being very competitive regarding existing approaches. Both methods could benefit from improvements; ext-ZINBayes can be upgraded with the use of inference networks, whereas a new gene dispersion optimization mechanism may speed SIENA's inference. Another potential future work would be to integrate SIENA with some batch removal method designed specifically for scRNA data, in order to compute the Bayes factors without constraining the cell pairs by batch. One option is to employ batch correction by matching mutual nearest neighbors. Finally, both models can be used to devise some fold-change metric, possibly generating more accurate DE scores.

References

1. Anders, S., Huber, W.: Differential expression analysis for sequence count data. Genome Biol. **11**(10), R106 (2010)
2. Ashburner, M., Ashburner, M., et al.: Gene ontology: tool for the unification of biology. Nat. Genet. **25**(1), 25 (2000)
3. Blei, D.M., Kucukelbir, A., McAuliffe, J.D.: Variational inference: a review for statisticians. J. Am. Stat. Assoc. **112**(518), 859–877 (2017)
4. Dal Molin, A., Baruzzo, G., Di Camillo, B.: Single-cell RNA-sequencing: assessment of differential expression analysis methods. Front. Gen. **8**, 62 (2017)
5. Edgar, R.: Gene expression omnibus: NCBI gene expression and hybridization array data repository. NAR **30**(1), 207–210 (2002)
6. Ferreira, P.F., Carvalho, A.M., Vinga, S.: Scalable probabilistic matrix factorization for single-cell RNA-seq analysis (2018)
7. Finak, G., et al.: MAST: a flexible statistical framework for assessing transcriptional changes and characterizing heterogeneity in single-cell RNA sequencing data. Genome Biol. **16**(1), 278 (2015)
8. Islam, S., et al.: Characterization of the single-cell transcriptional landscape by highly multiplex RNA-seq. Genome Res. **21**(7), 1160–1167 (2011)
9. Kass, R.E., Raftery, A.E.: Bayes factors. J. Am. Stat. Assoc. **90**(430), 773–795 (1995)
10. Kharchenko, P.V., Silberstein, L., Scadden, D.T.: Bayesian approach to single-cell differential expression analysis. Nat. Methods **11**(7), 740–742 (2014)
11. Lopez, R., Regier, J., Cole, M.B., Jordan, M.I., Yosef, N.: Deep generative modeling for single-cell transcriptomics. Nat. Methods **15**(12), 1053 (2018)
12. Mar, J.C., et al.: Variance of gene expression identifies altered network constraints in neurological disease. PLoS Genet. **7**(8), e1002207 (2011)
13. Moliner, A., Ernfors, P., Ibáñez, C.F., Andäng, M.: Mouse embryonic stem cell-derived spheres with distinct neurogenic potentials. Stem Cells Dev **17**(2), 233–243 (2008)
14. Robinson, M.D., McCarthy, D.J., Smyth, G.K.: edgeR: a bioconductor package for differential expression analysis of digital gene expression data. Bioinformatics **26**(1), 139–140 (2009)
15. Smyth, G.K.: Linear models and empirical bayes methods for assessing differential expression in microarray experiments. Stat. Appl. Genet. Mol. Biol. **3**(1), 1–25 (2004)

Computational Advances for Single-Cell Omics Data Analysis

Computational Cell Cycle Analysis of Single Cell RNA-Seq Data

Marmar Moussa[1]($\boxtimes$) and Ion I. Măndoiu[2]

[1] School of Medicine, University of Connecticut, Farmington, CT, USA
marmar.moussa@uconn.edu
[2] University of Connecticut, Storrs, CT, USA
ion@engr.uconn.edu

Abstract. The variation in gene expression profiles of cells captured in different phases of the cell cycle can interfere with cell type identification and functional analysis of single cell RNA-Seq (scRNA-Seq) data. In this paper, we introduce SC1CC (**SC1 C**ell **C**ycle analysis tool), a computational approach for clustering and ordering single cell transcriptional profiles according to their progression along cell cycle phases. We also introduce a new robust metric, Gene Smoothness Score (GSS) for assessing the cell cycle based order of the cells. SC1CC is available as part of the SC1 web-based scRNA-Seq analysis pipeline, publicly accessible at https://sc1.engr.uconn.edu/.

Keywords: scRNA-Seq · Cell cycle · Cell order · Gene smoothness score

1 Background and Motivation

The variation in gene expression profiles of single cells that are captured in different phases of the cell cycle can interfere with cell type identification and functional analysis of single cell transcriptomic data. In particular, it is important to differentiate between cell type and cell cycle effects when analyzing single cell RNA-Seq data. A first challenge in the computational analysis of cell cycle effects in single cell transcriptomics is to differentiate between cells that are actively proliferating and those that are quiescent, i.e., cells that do not actively divide but retain the ability to re-enter a proliferative state. A second computational challenge is to correctly label individual cells or cell clusters according to their phase in the cell cycle. The main cell cycle phases are G1 (where metabolic changes prepare the cell for division), S (where DNA synthesis replicates the genetic material), G2 (where molecular components needed for mitosis and cytokinesis are assembled), and M (where a nuclear division followed by cytokinesis occurs), although transition phases G1/S and G2/M are also commonly identified [4]. Such cell labels coupled with existing biological knowledge of genes associated with each of the cell cycle phases can assist functional analysis of single cell

© Springer Nature Switzerland AG 2021
S. K. Jha et al. (Eds.): ICCABS 2020, LNBI 12686, pp. 71–87, 2021.
https://doi.org/10.1007/978-3-030-79290-9_7

transcriptional profiles and interpretation of unsupervised scRNA-Seq clustering results. Finally, a third computational challenge is to order individual cells according to their progression along the cell cycle.

Although there are several existing methods for cell cycle analysis of single cell RNA-Seq data, most of them attempt to address one of the above-mentioned challenges in isolation. Our proposed SC1CC method enables a comprehensive analysis of the cell cycle effects that can be performed independently of cell type/functional annotation, hence avoiding hazardous manipulation of the single cell transcription data that could lead to misleading analysis results. Specifically, SC1CC can be used to distinguish proliferating from quiescent cells and provides the ability to annotate cell populations based on the cell cycle phase. Additionally, the cells are also ordered based on their progression along the cell cycle phases.

In the remainder of this section we briefly review some representative methods for individually addressing the above challenges in cell cycle analysis of scRNA-Seq.

ccRemover. The ccRemover tool [2] attempts to *remove* the cell-cycle effects from the single cell transcriptional profiles. This is done by identifying those principal components that, based on their loadings, capture mostly cell cycle effects in a low dimensional principal component analysis (PCA) projection of the scRNA-Seq data. Subtracting these components is expected to enhance gene expression variation due to differences in cell type. We performed an initial test to determine the effectiveness of ccRemover at removing cell cycle effects by running it with default settings on a dataset consisting of a 50%–50% mixture of Jurkat and 293T single cells that was previously profiled using the 10x Genomics droplet-based scRNA-Seq platform. This dataset is comprised of cells of two different types (T lymphocyte and human embryonic kidney cells) that are well separated according to their original scRNA-Seq profiles (Fig. 1a). However, after processing the scRNA-Seq data using ccRemover the two cell types appear nearly indistinguishable in the 3D t-SNE (t-Distributed Stochastic Neighbor Embedding) plot (Fig. 1b). This suggests that attempting to subtract the cell cycle signal using ccRemover without careful parameter tuning could result in inadvertently subtracting the cell type signal. For this reason, ccRemover was not included in further method comparisons in this paper.

Cyclone. Cyclone [16] uses a classification algorithm based on selecting pairs of genes whose relative expression has a sign that changes with the cell-cycle phase in the training data. The learned gene pairs are used to quantify the evidence that a given cell is in one of three cell cycle phases (G1, S, or G2M). Specifically, under the recommended approach, Cyclone calculates for each cell a score between 0 and 1 for two of these phases, G1 and G2M. Cells with G1 or G2M scores above 0.5 are assigned to the G1 or G2M phases, respectively (if both scores are above 0.5, then the higher score is used to make the assignment). Cells with both G1 and G2M scores below 0.5 are assigned by default to the S phase. The method allows users to override these thresholds, but we used

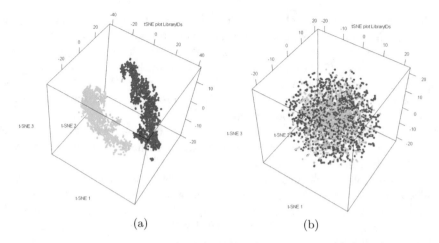

(a)   (b)

Fig. 1. ccRemover effect on data variability. (a) 3D t-SNE plot of Jurkat-239T data (Blue and red colors distinguish the Jurkat and 239T cells respectively). (b) 3D t-SNE plot of the Jurkat-293T dataset after applying ccRemover with default settings. As in [19] we inferred the cluster/library labels based on the expression of cell type-specific markers, The blue cluster corresponds to Jurkat cells (preferentially expressing CD3D), and red corresponds to 293T cells (preferentially expressing XIST, as 293T is a female cell line, while Jurkat is a male cell line).

the recommended thresholds in our experiments. In Sect. 3 we present results comparing the accuracy of cell cycle labels inferred by Cyclone to those generated by SC1CC using datasets with both known and unknown cell cycle phase labels.

reCAT. The reCAT method [12] takes a different approach to cell cycle analysis. Rather than labeling the cells with an inferred cell cycle phase, reCAT attempts to *order* the cells in a manner consistent to their position along the cell cycle. The cell ordering problem is computationally modeled as a traveling salesman problem (TSP). First, reCAT performs normalization of the data followed by clustering of the cells. It then orders the identified clusters by finding a traveling salesman cycle. It also computes for each cell two scores (a Bayes score and a mean score) that differentiate between the cell cycle phases. Finally, a hidden Markov model (HMM) and a Kalman smoother are used to estimate the underlying gene expression levels of the ordered single cells. The results of experiments comparing the order reconstructed by reCAT to the order identified by SC1CC are presented in Sect. 3.

2   Methods

2.1   Datasets

In addition to the Jurkat-239T dataset described in Sect. 1 we used four other datasets to further evaluate the performance of SC1CC and existing cell cycle analysis tools. These datasets were selected to span a broad range of cell cycle related modalities. For example, all cells in the Human Embryonic Stem Cells (hESC) dataset are expected to be proliferating, whereas the Peripheral blood mononuclear cells (PBMC) dataset is expected to consist solely of quiescent cells [19]. The immune cells from anti-CTLA-4 treated mice (α-CTLA-4) dataset and the mouse Hematopoietic Stem Cells (mHSC) are both expected to contain a mix of quiescent and proliferating cells.

The cells of the hESC dataset have labeled cell cycle phase annotations, while for the α-CTLA-4 and mHSC datasets only the percentage of proliferating cells was established in the original publications.

Basic quality control (QC) was uniformly applied to each of these datasets, whereby cells expressing less than 500 genes as well as genes detected in less than 10 cells were filtered out. Pre-processed versions of all datasets are accessible as example datasets for the SC1 web-based scRNA-Seq analysis pipeline [13], publicly available at https://sc1.engr.uconn.edu/.

Human Embryonic Stem Cells (hESC, Cycling Cells). There are very few scRNA-Seq datasets where the cell-cycle phase of each cell is known *a priori*. For this work, we used a labeled dataset of undifferentiated H1 human embryonic stem cells (hESCs) from [11]. Fluorescent ubiquitination-based cell-cycle indicator H1 (H1-Fucci) human embryonic stem cells were sorted according to the G1, S, and G2/M cell cycle phases by fluorescence activated cell sorting (FACS). Full-length scRNA-Seq data was generated for a total of 247 H1-Fucci cells (91 G1, 80 S, and 76 G2/M cells, respectively) captured using the Fluidigm C1 microfluidic platform.

Peripheral Blood Mononuclear Cells (PBMC, Non-cycling Cells). The PBMC dataset is comprised of a mixture of mature FACS-sorted dendritic cells, natural killer, B and T cells from a healthy donor from [19] and further analyzed in [14]. This dataset consists of 2,882 cells randomly sampled from seven PBMC sub-populations independently sorted by FACS. scRNA-Seq data for these cells was generated using the 10x Genomics droplet-based platform and the 3'-end v1 protocol, as described in [19]. Figure 2a shows a 3-dimensional *t-Distributed Stochastic Neighbor Embedding (t-SNE)* plot of the PBMC dataset and the breakdown into the seven cell types. Since PBMCs typically differentiate in the thymus or lymph nodes, this dataset is expected to contain only non-cycling cells.

Tumor Infiltrating Immune Cells from Anti-CTLA-4 Treated Mice (α-CTLA-4, Mixture of Cycling and Non-cycling Cells). This dataset (publicly available in the NCBI GEO database under accession GSM3371686) was also generated using the 3'-end v1 scRNA-Seq protocol on the 10x Genomics platform. CD45+ cells were sorted by FACS from cell suspensions of dissociated tumors excised from mice treated with 9D9, an anti-CTLA-4 antibody, as

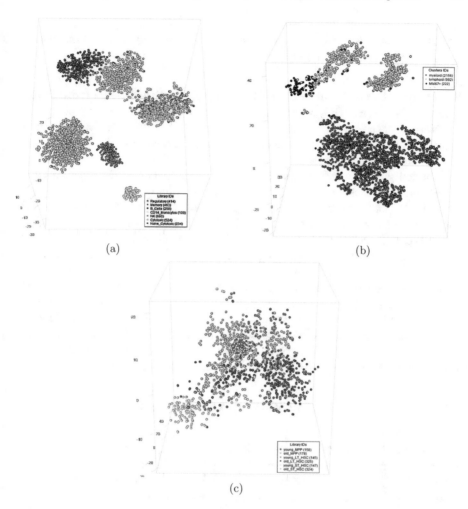

(a)   (b)

(c)

Fig. 2. 3-dimensional t-SNE plots of the PBMC, α-CTLA-4 and mHSC datasets. (a) 3D t-SNE plot of the 10x Genomics PBMC dataset consisting of 2,882 cells randomly sampled from seven PBMC sub-populations independently sorted by FACS. (b) 3D t-SNE plot of the α-CTLA-4 dataset consisting of 992 lymphoid (blue) and 2156 myeloid cells (red). The 'ki67-Hi' cells (black) are a mixture of proliferating CD4+ T cells, CD8+ T cells, Tregs, and NK cells (≈17.5% of the lymphoid cells). (c) 3D t-SNE plot of the mHSC dataset consisting of a total of 1,277 MPP, ST-HSC, and LT-HSC cells, further grouped by the age of the mice (young and old).

described in [7]. According to the analysis in [7], this dataset, henceforth referred to as α-CTLA-4, consists of 992 lymphoid and 2,156 myeloid cells. Notably, the unsupervised clustering analysis of the α-CTLA-4 dataset in [7] has identified a cluster, labeled 'Mki67-Hi', comprised of a mixture of proliferatingCD4+ T cells, CD8+ T cells, Tregs, and NK cells (≈17.5% of the lymphoid cells, see Fig. 2b). Thus, this dataset is well suited for assessing the ability of our method to correctly differentiate between quiescent and proliferating cells.

Short- and Long-Term Mouse Hematopoietic Stem Cells from Young and Old Mice (mHSC, Mixture of Cycling and Non-cycling Cells). This scRNA-seq dataset (1,277 cells after applying QC) is publicly available in the NCBI GEO database under accession GSE59114. The dataset was used in [9] to dissect the variability in hematopoietic stem cell (HSC) and hematopoietic progenitor cell populations from young and old mice. A 3D t-SNE projection of the mHSC dataset is shown in Fig. 2c. Based on the analysis in [9], this dataset is comprised of cells of three different types – Multipotent Progenitor Cells (MPP), short-term hematopoietic stem cell (ST-HSC), and long-term hematopoietic stem cell (LT-HSC) – that are further grouped by the age of the mice (young and old). The six cell populations are thoroughly analyzed in [9] with regards to cell cycle effect on differentiation while aging. We use the findings of this analysis as the ground truth for evaluating the performance of our approach. Specifically, the computational and biological analysis in [9] identifies 65% of all cells analyzed as non-dividing and estimates an equal percentage of proliferating cells in young and old mice for MPP and ST-HSC cells but not for LT-HSCs (of which old mice have fewer dividing cells). The analysis in [9] also estimates the percentages of cells in G1, S and G2M phases as 20%, 6% and 9% of the total, respectively.

2.2 The SC1 Cell Cycle (SC1CC) Analysis Tool

A repeated observation in single cell RNA-Seq data analysis is that a bias can be introduced by cell cycle effects. Indeed, such effects result in significant factor loadings of annotated cell cycle genes to the first few principal components for many scRNA-Seq datasets. Furthermore, it has been shown that the first few principal components obtained by using expression levels of annotated cell cycle genes are sufficient for capturing cell to cell similarities and the covariance due to cell cycle effects [2,3,5,11,16]. We leverage this observation in SC1CC and start by computing the first few principal components (PCs) for the sub-matrix of normalized scRNA-Seq counts comprised of cell cycle genes only.

The SC1CC implementation available at https://sc1.engr.uconn.edu/ allows users to select one of three different gene lists: the genes annotated with the "cell cycle" term (GO:0007049) in the Gene Ontology database [6], genes included in the Cyclebase 3.0 database of cell cycle related genes [15], and finally the list of periodic genes identified from single cell data in [5]. All results in this paper are based on the GO-annotated cell cycle gene unless otherwise indicated. The selected list of cell cycle genes is further filtered based on the gene expression values in the current dataset in order to keep only those expressed genes that have a correlation higher than α to at least one other cell cycle gene. The purpose of this step is to remove genes that – although annotated as cell cycle genes – do not have expression levels correlated with that of other cell cycle genes, and hence might represent outliers. All experiments reported in Sect. 3 were generated using the default value of 0.25 for α.

Since using a large number of PCs can add unnecessary noise to subsequent analysis steps, by default SC1CC automatically determines the number of relevant PCs by assessing the drop in variance explained for each pair of consecutive principal components. The online SC1CC implementation allows users to manually specify the number of PCs if desired. The principal component analysis is followed in SC1CC by a 3-dimensional t-SNE projection using the identified principal components. Performing t-SNE based dimensionality reduction using the main PCs aims to capture the local similarity of the cells without sacrificing the global variation already captured by the PC analysis. Next, the cells – now identified by their representation in t-SNE space – are clustered into a hierarchical structure (dendrogram) based on their Cosine similarity. Unless otherwise indicated all results reported in the paper are based on using hierarchical clustering with average linkage; the online SC1CC implementation also allows users to select between average linkage and Ward's method.

Since the cell cycle is typically divided into 6 distinct phases (G1, G1/S, S, G2, G2/M, and M, see, e.g., [4]), by default SC1CC attempts to extract up to 7 clusters from the hierarchical clustering dendogram – corresponding to the 6 cell cycle phases plus at least one potential cluster of non-cycling cells – with a minimum cluster size threshold of 25 cells. The maximum number of clusters can be modified by the user in the online implementation of SC1CC, which also includes an 'auto' option for determining the optimal number of clusters based on the Gap Statistics Analysis algorithm from [17].

Finally, to generate an order of cells consistent to their position along the cell cycle, SC1CC reorders the leaves of the hierarchical clustering dendogram (corresponding to the individual cells) by using the *Optimal Leaf Ordering (OLO)* algorithm [1] as implemented in [8]. Performing additional leaf-node reordering is equivalent to minimizing the length of a Hamiltonian path [1]. For n cells, the dendrogram produced by the hierarchical clustering algorithm (essentially a rooted binary tree) has $n - 1$ internal nodes and 2^{n-1} possible leaf orderings. That is, at each internal node the left and right subtrees can be independently flipped or not. The OLO algorithm produces a leaf ordering that minimizes the sum of distances between adjacent leaves. The time complexity of the implementation in [8] is $O(n^3)$, and its practical performance as part of SC1CC is further improved since the pairwise distances between cells are already available from the distance based hierarchical clustering step.

Cluster Mean-Scores. Six groups of genes (G1, G1/S, S, G2, G2/M, and M genes, respectively) are formed by including cell cycle genes that are known to reach their peak expression in the corresponding cell cycle phases [12]. For each of these genes and each cell, a 'z-score' is computed by subtracting the gene's mean expression level from the expression level of the gene in the cell and then dividing by the gene's standard deviation. For each group of genes and each cluster identified during the hierarchical clustering step we compute a mean-score by averaging over cells in the cluster and genes in the group. The maximum mean-score of a cluster is used to determine its cell cycle phase. Note that with this procedure multiple clusters can be labeled with the same cell cycle phase, and some cell cycle phases may not be assigned as labels to any of the clusters. Also, since a mean-score of each gene group corresponding to each of the cell cycle phases can be calculated for each identified cluster, the maximum mean-score is relative between gene groups of different cell cycle phases and can only indicate a potential cell cycle phase designation. We therefore introduce in next sub-section an independent metric that can be used to distinguish dividing from non-dividing cells.

Gene-Smoothness Score (GSS). Normalized gene scores computed as above or as defined by reCAT [12] or Cyclone [16] are relative between cell cycle phases and cannot distinguish clearly, if at all, between cycling vs. non-cycling cells or provide a useful metric for assessing cell orderings. We therefore propose a novel metric, referred to as Gene-Smoothness Score (GSS), based on serial correlation, i.e., the correlation between a given variable and a lagged version of itself. The GSS can be computed for any ordered group of cells and can help to directly assess the suggested cell order. Strengths of this metric include the fact that the cells do not need to have known cell-cycle labels and that no specific model assumptions are required for the marker gene expression (whether binary, bimodal, sinusoidal, etc.). Our experiments also indicate that the GSS results are relatively insensitive to the choice of annotated cell cycle genes, hence the GSS can be useful even when a "perfect" annotation is not available.

The GSS of an ordered cluster/group c of cells is defined as

$$GSS(c) = Median \left\{ \left| SC_{ord}(g_i) - \frac{1}{R} \sum_{j=1}^{R} SC_{rand_j}(g_i) \right| \ : \ i = 1, \ldots, N \right\} \quad (1)$$

where N is the number of annotated cell cycle genes, $SC_{ord}(g_i)$ denotes the first-order serial correlation of gene i with respect to the given cell order, and $SC_{rand_j}(g_i)$, $j = 1, \ldots, R$, denote the first-order serial correlation of gene i with respect to R randomized cell orders (we use $R = 50$ in all experiments). The first-order serial (or auto-) correlation is the correlation value between a given gene expression vector and a version of itself shifted by one position. Serial correlation is a value between -1 and 1. First-order serial correlation near 0 implies that there is no overall correlation between adjacent data points. On the other hand, a first-order serial correlation near 1 suggests a smoothly varying series, while a first-order serial correlations near -1 indicates a series that alternates between high and low values. Because individual cell cycle genes can be expressed in different patterns throughout the cell cycle phase transitions, and even abruptly switch direction when the assessed cluster includes mostly cells in one of the transient cell cycle phases (G1/S or G2/M), we define GSS as the median (over all cell cycle genes) of the absolute differences between the serial correlation of a gene's expression values ordered according to the given cell ordering and the average serial correlation computed over R randomized orders.

A cluster/group of cells is considered to be cycling/dividing when its GSS is greater than an error margin ε (default 0.05), i.e., when at least 50% of the genes have an absolute difference in serial correlations between randomized order and identified cell cycle order of at least 0.05. The value of the error margin is set to 0.05 by default but can be adjusted by the user in the online SC1CC implementation. The GSS score is more robust with a higher number of cells per cell cycle cluster, as the chance of a random order producing spurious auto-correlation and therefore high GSS scores is lower when more data points are included in the series.

Figure 3 provides examples of cell cycle genes that contribute positive values to the GSS score in the hESC dataset and illustrates their expression values for both SC1CC and randomly ordered cells. The online implementation of SC1CC allows the user to select any cell cycle gene of interest and examine its normal-ized expression levels along the inferred order. In Figure 3, gray dots represent normalized gene expression values for individual cells, while the red and blue curves represent the fitted local polynomial regression of these values for the SC1CC and a random cell order, respectively. As expected, the fitted expression lines under random ordering of the cells convey no recognizable pattern and stay nearly flat close to an altitude of 0. In contrast, the SC1CC cell order results in fitted curves that appear to peak at different positions, consistent with these gene's involvement in different cell cycle phases.

3   Results and Discussion

3.1   Results on the hESC Dataset

The cell order inferred by SC1CC's OLO algorithm and the cell cycle order reconstructed by reCAT are shown in Fig. 4a. SC1CC groups together almost

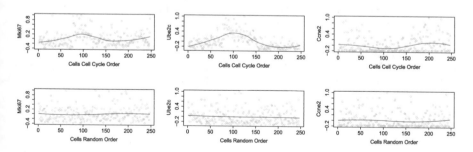

Fig. 3. Example cell cycle genes in the hESC dataset. Normalized expression levels for select cell cycle genes and cells ordered by SC1CC (red) vs. a shuffled cells order (blue). Different cell cycle genes follow different patterns of expression along the cell cycle phases. Given the SC1CC inferred cell order, which reflects the cells' progression through the cell cycle, different patterns for individual cell cycle genes can be seen for different genes associated with the cell cycle, including Mki67, Ube2c, Ccne2

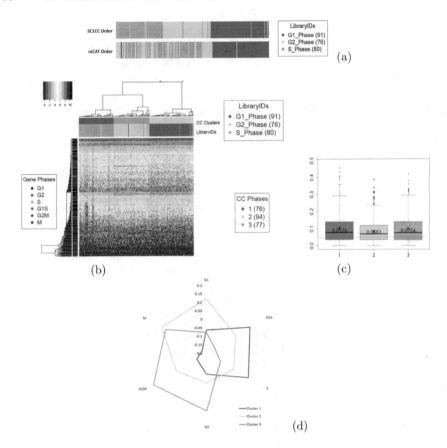

Fig. 4. Cell cycle analysis of the hESC dataset. (a) hESC cells orders inferred by SC1CC and reCAT. Experimentally determined cell labels are color coded as library IDs. SC1CC groups the majority of cells from each phase together (G1 in red, G2 in blue, and S in orange), whereas only G1 cells are grouped together in the reCAT order. (b) Heatmap of $log_2(x+1)$ expression values of cell cycle genes for the hESC cells using 'GO:0007049' gene list ordered according to SC1CC. Colors in the top bar labeled 'CC Clusters' represent the identified cell cycle clusters according to SC1CC, whereas the colors in the 'Library IDs' bar of the heat map indicate the cell cycle phases determined by FACS. (c) GSS for the three clusters identified by running SC1CC on the hESC cells. (d) Mean-scores for each of the three clusters identified by SC1CC and each of the six considered cell cycle phases.

all cells labeled with the same phase. Although the reCAT order maintains the grouping of G1 cells, cells from S and G2 phases are highly interleaved in this order. The SC1CC order also has a higher GSS score of 0.0632 compared to 0.0519 for the reCAT order.

Figure 4b displays the heat map of $log_2(x+1)$ expression values of cell cycle genes for the hESC cells ordered according to SC1CC. Colors in the top bar labeled 'CC Clusters' represent the identified cell cycle clusters according to SC1CC, whereas the colors in the 'Library IDs' bar of the heat map indicate in this case the cell cycle phases determined by FACS. Note that the colors for library IDs and inferred cell cycle clusters are assigned independently from the same color palette in our online implementation and therefore are not necessarily in one-to-one correspondence. The heat map in Fig. 4b was generated by running SC1CC using the set of genes associated with the GO term "Cell Cycle" (GO:0007049). The hierarchical clustering algorithm implemented by SC1CC identifies three clusters. The GSS scores (Fig. 4c) for the three clusters were 0.0775, 0.0683, and 0.0754, respectively, indicating that all clusters consist of dividing cells, as expected.

Figure 4d gives the mean scores for each of the three clusters identified by SC1CC and each of the six considered cell cycle phases. Based on majority matching of cell labels determined by FACS, the three clusters are comprised of cells in the S, G1, and G2 phases, respectively. Albeit not perfect, the cluster assignments based on peak mean scores have good agreement. Specifically, cluster 1 (consisting of S phase cells according to the FACS labels) has very close highest mean scores for the G1S and S phases, with the G1S score slightly higher. Cluster 2 (G1 according to FACS) has two close highest scores for G1 and M phases, with the G1 score slightly higher. Finally, cluster 3 (G2 according to FACS) has two close highest mean scores for the G2 and G2M phases, with the G2M score slightly higher. The relatively low number of cells as well as the limited resolution of the ground truth labels are both likely contributing factors to the near-ties in peak score assignments for the three clusters.

In Table 1 we compare the clusters (cell labels) generated by Cyclone with the clusters inferred by SC1CC using different cell cycle gene sets for the hESC dataset. We assess clustering accuracy using the macro and micro-accuracy measures from [10] and [18], defined as:

$$Micro\,Accuracy = \sum_{i=1}^{K} C_i / \sum_{i=1}^{K} N_i \qquad (2)$$

$$Macro\,Accuracy = \frac{1}{K} \sum_{i=1}^{K} \frac{C_i}{N_i} \qquad (3)$$

where K is the number of classes, N_i is the size of class i, and C_i is the number of correctly labeled samples in class i relative to the ground truth.

Both Cyclone and SC1CC cluster the cells with high accuracy, with Cyclone scoring slightly higher. As detailed in Sect. 2.2, SC1CC gives the user the choice to use three different lists: genes included in the Cyclebase 3.0 database [15], genes annotated with the "cell cycle" term (GO:0007049) in the Gene Ontology database [6], and the list of periodic genes identified from single cell data in [5]. As can be seen in Table 1, the genes associated to the term "Cell Cycle" (GO:0007049) from the The Gene Ontology (GO) database achieve slightly higher clustering micro- and macro-accuracy for the hESC dataset compared to the other two gene sets.

Table 1. Clustering accuracy for Cyclone and SC1CC run with three different gene lists on the hESC dataset.

	Cyclone	SC1CC		
		Cyclebase 3.0	GO	Periodic Genes
G1-Phase	**1.000**	0.9890	0.9890	**1.000**
G2-Phase	0.9342	0.7895	**0.9605**	0.8290
S-Phase	**1.000**	**1.000**	0.9125	0.9875
Micro accuracy	**0.9798**	0.9312	0.9555	0.9433
Macro accuracy	**0.9781**	0.9262	0.9540	0.9388

3.2   Results on the PBMC Dataset

As described in Sect. 2.1, the PBMC dataset is expected to include mostly non-dividing cells, which is confirmed by the results of the SC1CC analysis. Figure 5a shows the heat map of the PBMC cells featuring the GO cell cycle related genes that are expressed in the dataset (using $log_2(x+1)$ expression) and the clustering obtained by SC1CC. The majority of the genes have low expression levels in most cells. Furthermore, the GSS scores of all clusters fall below the 0.05 cutoff and hence they are all labeled as non-dividing by SC1CC (Fig. 5b), as expected. Cyclone labels 2,192 of the 2,882 cells in the PBMC dataset as G1, 398 as G2M, and 292 as S phase cells, underscoring the need for a separate analysis step to determine if the cells are actually cycling.

3.3   Results on the α-CTLA-4 Dataset

As discussed in Sect. 2.1, the α-CTLA-4 dataset is expected to include a mix of dividing and non-dividing cells. This is the most likely scenario for many scRNA-Seq datasets where no knowledge of the cell cycle effect within the data is available *a priori*. We reasoned that the best analysis approach for such data is to perform a two stage analysis, where we first separate the dividing from the non-dividing cells, followed by a detailed cell cycle analysis of the potentially dividing cells identified in the first step. Indeed, after clustering and ordering the cells using SC1CC, we are able to distinguish the potentially dividing cells by their GSS score. Figure 6a shows the $log_2(x+1)$ expression heat map of the 3,148 α-CTLA-4 cells passing the default QC described in Sect. 2.1 based on the GO cell cycle genes and using the first 4 principal components. One cluster (cluster 7 in light green color) consists of 193 cells that show markedly higher expression levels for the cell cycle genes. Independent clustering analysis based on full gene expression profiles performed using the SC1 pipeline shows that cluster 7 is comprised mostly of lymphoid cells (light blue in the horizontal bar labeled "Clusters" in the heat map). This cluster has the highest GSS score, exceeding the SC1CC detection threshold for dividing cells, as shown in Fig. 6b. Indeed, this cluster closely matches the "Mki67-Hi" cluster identified in [7] as

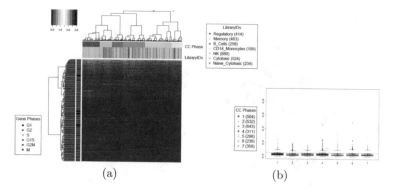

(a)   (b)

Fig. 5. Cell cycle analysis of the PBMC dataset. Heat map and cell order (a) along with GSS scores for the clusters inferred by SC1CC (b) on the PBMC dataset. GSS scores for all clusters fall below a cutoff of 0.05 and are labeled as non-dividing by SC1CC.

consisting of highly proliferative lymphoid cells. Further SC1CC analysis of the 193 cells in this cluster based on the Cyclebase 3.0 gene list reveals three sub-clusters (Fig. 6c), all of which are found to be actively dividing according to GSS scores (Fig. 6d). Cell cycle phase assignments based on maximum mean-scores suggests that the three sub-clusters consist of cells in the M, S, and G1S phases, respectively (Fig. 6e). For the sake of completeness we also tested Cyclone classification method on the of the 3,148 α-CTLA-4 cells, and 2,957 cells were labeled as G1, 149 were labeled as G2M, and 42 were labeled as S phase cells.

3.4   Results on the mHSC Dataset

As discussed in Sect. 2.1, this dataset also includes a mix of dividing and non-dividing cells. As with the α-CTLA-4 dataset analysis, we followed a two stage SC1CC analysis approach, where we first separate the dividing from the non-dividing cells, followed by a detailed cell cycle analysis of the potentially dividing cells identified in the first step. In excellent agreement with the percentages reported in [9], the first analysis stage (Fig. 7a–b) places 472 of the 1,277 mHSC cells (36.96%) in a dividing cluster with GSS score of 0.3075, and the remaining cells in a non-dividing cluster with GSS score of 0.0285. Furthermore, as shown in Table 2, the percentage of dividing cells identified by SC1CC among the three cell types identified in [9] are indeed approximately equal in young and old mice, with the exception of long term HSC, only 13% of which are dividing in old mice compared to 35% in young mice.

The analysis in [9] 'roughly' estimates the percentage of cells in G1, G1/S and G2M phases as 20%, 6% and 9% respectively. Following the second stage of analysis, where cycling cells identified in first stage are further clustered and assigned cell cycle phases based on peak mean scores (Fig. 7c–e), SC1CC identifies 217 cells (17% of total) as G1, 68 cells as G1/S (5.3% of total), and 187 cells as G2M (14.6% of total).

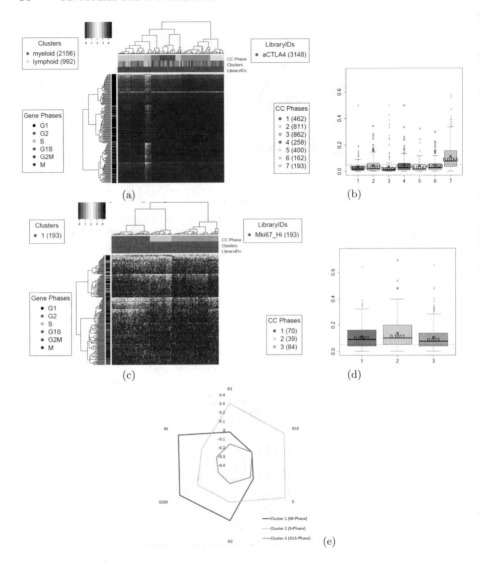

Fig. 6. Cell cycle analysis of the α-CTLA-4 dataset. Heat map and cell order (a) along with GSS scores for the clusters inferred by SC1CC (b) on the α-CTLA-4 dataset. The 193 cells in cluster 7 are further partitioned by SC1CC into 3 sub-clusters (c), all of which are marked as actively dividing based on GSS scores (d). Mean-scores for each of the three sub-clusters of dividing cells and each of the six considered cell cycle phases are given in (e). Mean-scores for each of the three sub-clusters of dividing cells and each of the six considered cell cycle phases are given in (e). The maximum mean-scores of sub-clusters 1 (red), 2 (blue), and 3 (orange) are achieved for the M, S, and G1/S phases, respectively.

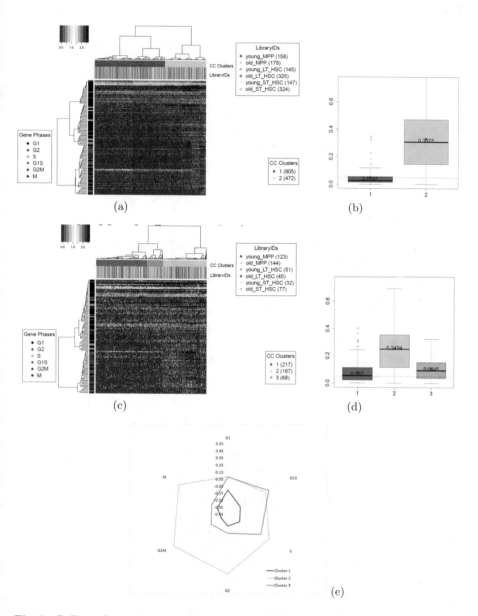

Fig. 7. Cell cycle analysis of the mHSC dataset. Heat map and cell order (a) along with GSS scores for the clusters inferred by SC1CC (b) on the mHSC dataset. The 472 cells in cluster 2 are further partitioned by SC1CC into 3 sub-clusters (c), all of which are marked as actively dividing based on GSS scores (d). Mean-scores for each of the three sub-clusters of dividing cells and each of the six considered cell cycle phases are given in (e). The maximum mean-scores of sub-clusters 1 (red), 2 (blue), and 3 (orange) are achieved for the G1, G2M, and G1/S phases, respectively.

Table 2. The inferred numbers of dividing vs. non-dividing cells in the six cell populations of the mHSC dataset.

	Non-Dividing	Dividing	% Dividing
Old mice MPP	34	144	80%
Young mice MPP	35	123	78%
Old mice ST-HSC	247	77	24%
Young mice ST-HSC	115	32	22%
Old mice LT-HSC	280	45	13%
Young mice LT-HSC	94	51	35%

4   Conclusion

In this paper we introduce SC1CC, a novel method for clustering and ordering single cell transcriptional profiles according to their cell cycle phase. The main contributions include a novel technique for ordering cells based on hierarchical clustering and optimal leaf ordering, and a new GSS metric based on serial correlation for assessing gene expression change smoothness along a reconstructed cell order as well as differentiating between cycling and non-cycling groups of cells. While many of the existing methods focus on a specific aspect of scRNA-Seq cell cycle analysis (e.g., assigning phase labels, ordering the cells, or removing the cell cycle contribution to gene expression), SC1CC is, to our best knowledge, the first method that enables a comprehensive analysis of the cell cycle effects, addressing four complementary analysis aspects. SC1CC differentiates between dividing and non-dividing cells, clusters the cells based on cell cycle effects independently from cell type effects, while also assigning cell cycle phases to the resulting clusters and ordering the cells based on their progression along the cell cycle phases. SC1CC has been implemented in R and deployed via a user-friendly interactive interface as part of the SC1 scRNA-Seq analysis pipeline [13], freely accessible at https://sc1.engr.uconn.edu/.

Empirical evaluation experiments on a diverse set of real scRNA-Seq datasets show that the GSS robust evaluation metric which allows distinguishing with high accuracy between dividing and non-dividing cells based on minimal assumptions about the underlying cell cycle gene expression changes. In direct comparisons with the existing specialized tools, SC1CC also achieves similar or better accuracy for clustering the cells according to cell cycle phases or ordering them according to the progression along the cell cycle phases. Importantly, SC1CC analysis is performed orthogonally to cell type identification, avoiding potentially artifacts of sequential analysis advocated in [2].

Acknowledgments. This work was partially supported by NSF Award 1564936, NIH grants 1R01MH112739-01 and R01NS073425, and a UConn Academic Vision Program Grant.

References

1. Bar-Joseph, Z., Gifford, D.K., Jaakkola, T.S.: Fast optimal leaf ordering for hierarchical clustering. Bioinformatics **17**(suppl_1), S22–S29 (2001)
2. Barron, M., Li, J.: Identifying and removing the cell-cycle effect from single-cell RNA-sequencing data. Sci. Rep. **6** (2016)
3. Buettner, F., et al.: Computational analysis of cell-to-cell heterogeneity in single-cell RNA-sequencing data reveals hidden subpopulations of cells. Nat. Biotechnol. **33**(2), 155–160 (2015)
4. Cooper, G.M., Hausman, R.E., Hausman, R.E.: The Cell: A Molecular Approach, vol. 10. ASM Press, Washington DC (2000)
5. Dominguez, D., Tsai, Y.H., Gomez, N., Jha, D.K., Davis, I., Wang, Z.: A high-resolution transcriptome map of cell cycle reveals novel connections between periodic genes and cancer. Cell Res. **26**(8), 946 (2016)
6. Gene Ontology Consortium: the gene ontology (GO) database and informatics resource. Nucleic Acids Res. **32**(suppl_1), D258–D261 (2004)
7. Gubin, M.M., Alspach, E., et al.: High-dimensional analysis delineates myeloid and lymphoid compartment remodeling during successful immune-checkpoint cancer therapy. Cell **175**(4), 1014–1030 (2018)
8. Hahsler, M., Hornik, K., Buchta, C.: Getting things in order: an introduction to the R package seriation. J. Stat. Softw. **25**(3), 1–34 (2008)
9. Kowalczyk, M.S.: Single-cell RNA-seq reveals changes in cell cycle and differentiation programs upon aging of hematopoietic stem cells. Genome Res. **25**(12), 1860–1872 (2015)
10. Lee, C., Măndoiu, I.I., Nelson, C.E.: Inferring ethnicity from mitochondrial DNA sequence. In: BMC Proceedings. vol. 5, p. S11. BioMed Central (2011)
11. Leng, N., et al.: Oscope identifies oscillatory genes in unsynchronized single-cell RNA-seq experiments. Nat. Methods **12**(10), 947 (2015)
12. Liu, Z., et al.: Reconstructing cell cycle pseudo time-series via single-cell transcriptome data. Nat. Commun. **8**(1), 22 (2017)
13. Moussa, M., Măndoiu, I.I.: SC1: a tool for interactive web-based single cell RNA-seq data analysis. In: Cai, Z., Mandoiu, I., Narasimhan, G., Skums, P., Guo, X. (eds.) ISBRA 2020. LNCS, vol. 12304, pp. 389–397. Springer, Cham (2020). https://doi.org/10.1007/978-3-030-57821-3_39
14. Moussa, M., Mandoiu, I.: Single cell RNA-seq data clustering using TF-IDF based methods. BMC-Genomics **19**(Suppl 6), 569 (2018)
15. Santos, A., Wernersson, R., Jensen, L.J.: Cyclebase 3.0: a multi-organism database on cell-cycle regulation and phenotypes. Nucleic Acids Res., gku1092 (2014)
16. Scialdone, A., et al.: Computational assignment of cell-cycle stage from single-cell transcriptome data. Methods **85**, 54–61 (2015)
17. Tibshirani, R., Walther, G., Hastie, T.: Estimating the number of clusters in a data set via the gap statistic. J. Royal Stat. Society Ser. B (Stat. Methodol.) **63**(2), 411–423 (2001)
18. Van Asch, V.: Macro-and micro-averaged evaluation measures. Technical report (2013)
19. Zheng, G.X.Y., et al.: Massively parallel digital transcriptional profiling of single cells. Nat. Commun. **8**, 14049 (2017)

Single-Cell Gene Regulatory Network Analysis Reveals Potential Mechanisms of Action of Antimalarials Against SARS-CoV-2

James J. Cai[1,2(✉)] ⓘ and Daniel Osorio[1] ⓘ

[1] Department of Veterinary Integrative Biosciences, Texas A&M University, College Station, TX 77843, USA
jcai@tamu.edu
[2] Department of Electrical and Computer Engineering, Texas A&M University, College Station, TX 77843, USA

Abstract. The efficiency of antimalarials, chloroquine (CQ) and hydroxychloroquine (HCQ), in the prevention and treatment of coronavirus disease 2019 (COVID-19) is under intense debate. The mechanisms of action of antimalarials against severe acute respiratory syndrome coronavirus 2 (SARS-CoV-2) have not been fully elucidated. Here, we applied a network-based comparative analysis, implemented in our machine learning workflow—scTenifoldNet, to scRNA-seq data from COVID-19 patients with different levels of severity. We found that genes of the Malaria pathway expressed in macrophages are significantly differentially regulated between patients with moderate and severe symptoms. Our findings help reveal the mechanisms of action of CQ and HCQ during SARS-CoV-2 infection, providing new evidence to support the use of these antimalarial drugs in the treatment of COVID-19, especially for patients who are mildly affected or in the early stage of the infection.

Keywords: scRNA-seq · Machine learning · Gene regulatory network · scTenifoldNet · SARS-CoV-2 · Antimalarial · Hydroxychloroquine

1 Introduction

The efficiency of chloroquine (CQ) and hydroxychloroquine (HCQ) in the prevention and treatment of coronavirus disease 2019 (COVID-19) is under intense debate [1–5]. HCQ is the hydroxylated derivative of CQ; both are weak bases with a common flat aromatic core structure and proven antimalarial drugs. HCQ is also widely used as an immunomodulator to treat autoimmune diseases, especially systemic lupus erythematosus (SLE) and rheumatoid arthritis (RA) [6]. CQ and HCQ are considered potent candidates to treat infection of severe acute respiratory syndrome coronavirus 2 (SARS-CoV-2)—the etiological agent of the COVID-19 [7, 8]. Experimental studies suggest that CQ and HCQ have the capability of inhibiting the replication of several intracellular micro-organisms [9], including SARS-CoV-2 *in vitro* [10, 11]. Several human studies have been conducted with both these drugs in COVID-19, and have shown significant

© Springer Nature Switzerland AG 2021
S. K. Jha et al. (Eds.): ICCABS 2020, LNBI 12686, pp. 88–94, 2021.
https://doi.org/10.1007/978-3-030-79290-9_8

improvement in some parameters in patients with COVID-19 [3, 12]. Although the use of CQ and HCQ in COVID-19 treatment has been recommended, the link between the mechanism of action of antimalarials and the mechanism of SARS-CoV-2 cellular infection is still missing. Without the link being established, how CQ and HCQ act against SARS-CoV-2 will remain elusive.

2 Materials and Methods

2.1 Data Set

We downloaded a published single-cell RNA sequencing (scRNA-seq) data set [13] to perform a transcriptomic comparative analysis between COVID-19 patients with moderate and severe symptoms. The scRNA-seq data was collected from cells in bronchoalveolar lavage fluid (BALF) from three patients with moderate and six patients with severe infection symptoms [13]. We downloaded the raw data from the Sequence Read Archive (SRA) database using accession number SRP250732 and processed the data to generate scRNA-seq expression matrices. In the scRNA-seq data analysis, cells from patients with moderate (M) and severe (S) symptoms were pooled into M and S groups for comparison. After performing the data quality control and cell clustering, we extracted 1,125 and 3,735 macrophages from cells of M and S groups, respectively (Fig. 1a). The identity of macrophages was confirmed with marker genes including *CD68* (Fig. 1b). We chose to focus on macrophages due to the abundance of cells in the samples (77.4% of cells are macrophages in the data) and the importance of lung macrophages contributing to local inflammation, including recruiting inflammatory monocytic cells and neutrophils and attracting T cells, as suggested in the original paper [13]. Toll-like receptor gene, *TLR2*, was found to be highly expressed among macrophages in the S group (Fig. 1c).

2.2 Machine Learning Workflow

To systematically compare macrophage transcriptomes between M and S patient groups, we employed a machine learning workflow—named scTenifoldNet (Fig. 1d), which we developed to construct and compare single-cell gene regulatory networks (scGRNs) [14]. scTenifoldNet is a machine learning framework that uses a comparative network approach with scRNA-seq data to identify regulatory changes between samples. scTenifoldNet is composed of five major steps. (1) *Cell subsampling*. scTenifoldNet starts with subsampling cells in the scRNA-seq expression matrices. Cells are subsampled either randomly or following a pseudotime trajectory of cells. The subsampling is repeated multiple times to create a series of subsampled cell populations. (2) *Network construction*. The subsampled data matrices are subject to network construction and form a multilayer single-cell gene regulatory network (scGRN). Principal component regression is used for network construction; each scGRN is represented as a weighted adjacency matrix. (3) *Tensor denoising*. The multilayer scGRN constructed from the subsampled data matrices is treated as a three-order tensor, which is subsequently decomposed into multiple components. Top components of tensor decomposition are then used to reconstruct denoised multilayer scGRN. The denoised multilayer scGRN is collapsed by taking average weight across layers. (4) *Manifold alignment*. Two denoised scGRNs: one from the first sample and the other from the other sample to be compared, are aligned with respect to common genes using a nonlinear manifold alignment algorithm. Each gene is projected to a low-rank manifold space as two data points, one from each sample. (5) *Differential regulation test*. The distance between the two data points is the relative difference of the gene in its regulatory relationships in the two scGRNs. Ranked genes are subject to tests for their significance in differential regulation between scGRNs. The most important advantage of this network-based comparative analytical framework is its sensitivity. We have shown that scTenifoldNet can detect differential regulatory patterns between highly similar scRNA-seq samples to reveal gene regulatory changes, which are undetectable otherwise [14].

3   Results and Discussion

We anticipated that, when applying scTenifoldNet to the scRNA-seq data of BALF from COVID-19 patients, we could decipher the molecular complexity of the data to achieve breakthroughs through constructing and comparing scGRNs in this cellular system affected by SARS-CoV-2. Indeed, scTenifoldNet took two expression matrices of M and S groups (containing 3,792 genes) as input and identified 27 highly differentially regulated genes [false discovery rate (FDR) < 0.05]: *BCAS4, ENO3, AD000091.1, JSRP1, SNX32, ATG10, NOP16, CR759762.1, SMPD4, BEST1, KCP, CR388220.1, DNAJC17,* **ABCB9**, *EME2, KIFC1, AL671277.1, UBXN11, CR759790.1, AL669813.2, BX005428.2, BOLA2,* **PPT1**, *SH3D19, OR7C1, MFSD11,* and *FKBP15* (Fig. 1e, genes are sorted according to the P-value significance; *PPT1* and *ABCB9* shown in bold are genes found in the *Lysosome* pathway of KEGG database). scTenifoldNet also generated a ranked list of genes, including the aforementioned 27 highly significant genes and all the rest of genes, sorted according to the significance of the scTenifoldNet test. We analyzed the ranked gene list using pre-ranked Gene Set Enrichment Analysis (GSEA), which is a method for determining whether any prior gene sets show statistical significance with respect to a ranked gene list. The results of GSEA analysis showed that eight pathway gene sets are highly significant (adjusted P-value < 0.05, Table 1). Among the eight, the most informative one is the *Malaria* pathway from the Kyoto Encyclopedia of Genes and Genomes (KEGG) database (Fig. 1e, inset). Thus, scTenifoldNet analysis suggested that genes in the Malaria pathway are significantly differentially regulated between M and S patient groups. We mapped expressed genes in our data set to the KEGG Malaria pathway and highlighted genes highly expressed in severe patients with red and lowly expressed with green (Fig. 1f). In the map, we found that *TLR2/4* and *TGFB*—two genes on the pathway leading to immunosuppression, and *CXCL8, MCP1,* and *IL1A*—genes known to participate in the development of fever and metabolic acidosis [15], are highly expressed in severely affected patients. Upregulated expression of *TLR2* in immune cells is also reported in patients affected with SLE [16], for which HCQ is a drug for treatment.

Given that our machine learning workflow identified that the *Malaria* pathway-related gene expression program is associated with different COVID-19 symptom severity, it is easy to conjure up the idea that antimalarials are potential candidates for treating early SARS-CoV-2 infection, especially when the symptom is less severe. Our reasoning is further supported by mechanisms of action of CQ and HCQ—modulate cellular immunity by suppressing immune cell function and reducing the secretion of pro-inflammation cytokines [6, 17]. This idea is also supported by several other pathway gene sets identified by scTenifoldNet, which are differentially regulated between M and S groups. These pathways include *Cellular response to type I interferon (GO:0071357)*, *Type I interferon signaling pathway (GO:0060337)*, *Antigen processing and presentation*, *Interferon alpha/beta signaling Homo sapiens R-HSA-909733*, and *Chemokine-mediated signaling pathway (GO:0070098)* (Table 1).

The significant pathway gene sets also include *Phagosome* and *Endosomal/Vacuolar pathway Homo sapiens R-HSA-1236977* (Table 1). These pathway gene sets, along with *PPT1* and *ABCB9*, the two highly significant genes that are also in the lysosome pathway, suggest that different levels of symptom severity between M and S groups may be associated with the lysosome function. These results further justify the use of CQ and HCQ for COVID-19 treatment. An important mode of action of CQ and HCQ is the inhibition of lysosomal activity [18]. CQ and HCQ are weak bases that are known

Table 1. Significant pathway gene sets identified using scTenifoldNet-ranked genes with GSEA analysis.

Pathway	P-value	Adjusted P-value	Size of gene set	Five representative genes (i.e., leading edges of GSEA)
Type I interferon signaling pathway (GO:0060337)	8.62E−07	0.002	37	*MX1, STAT1, ADAR, SAMHD1, OASL*
Antigen processing and presentation	2.34E−05	0.02	35	*IFI30, CD74, CTSB, HLA-DQA1, CTSL*
Malaria	1.57E−05	0.02	14	*CCL2, TLR2, LRP1, PECAM1, MYD88*
Phagosome	8.57E−05	0.02	71	*ACTB, HLA-DQA1, CTSL, HLA-C, TAP1*
Endosomal/Vacuolar pathway Homo sapiens R-HSA-1236977	4.55E−05	0.03	9	*CTSL, HLA-C, HLA-A, HLA-B, LNPEP*
Interferon alpha/beta signaling Homo sapiens R-HSA-909733	2.61E−05	0.03	38	*MX1, STAT1, ADAR, SAMHD1, OASL*
Chemokine-mediated signaling pathway (GO:0070098)	2.85E−05	0.04	9	*CCL2, CXCL10, CCL8, CCL7, CXCL11*
Cellular response to type I interferon (GO:0071357)	8.62E−07	0.002	37	*MX1, STAT1, ADAR, SAMHD1, OASL*

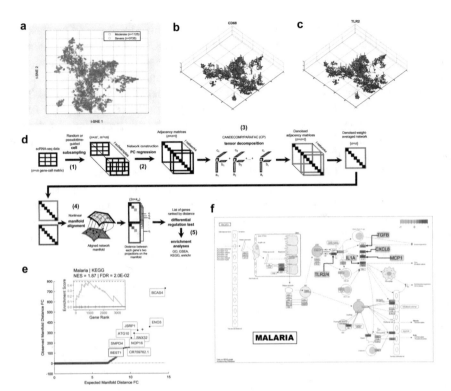

Fig. 1. Expression of genes in the Malaria pathway is differentially regulated in macrophages from COVID-19 patients with moderate and severe symptoms. (**a**) t-distributed stochastic neighbor embedding (t-SNE) plot of macrophages used in the data analysis. Cells are colored according to the group of COVID-19 patients: moderate (blue) and severe (red). (**b**) Gene expression level of CD68 indicated with bars (magenta) on t-SNE plot of cells. (**c**) Gene expression level of *TLR2*. (**d**) scTenifoldNet workflow. (**e**) The quantile-quantile (q-q) plot for genes sorted by the significance in the differential regulation test of scTenifoldNet. The expected and observed fold-changes (FCs) between the distance of each gene's two projections on the manifold and the average distance are shown. Inset: GSEA result of Malaria pathway. (**f**) The Malaria pathway in KEGG database is shown with genes differentially regulated and differentially expressed between COVID-19 patients with moderate and severe symptoms highlighted. Genes with expression is upregulated (or downregulated) in severely affected patients are highlighted in red (or green). Five key genes: *TLR2/4*, *TGFB*, *CXCL8* (i.e., *IL8*), *MCP1*, and *IL1A* (i.e., *IL1*), are further highlighted with an orange background in the pathway. A high-resolution image of this figure can be downloaded at https://github.com/cailab-tamu/covid19-antimalarials-letter/raw/master/Fig1.pdf.

to elevate the pH of acidic intracellular organelles, such as endosomes and lysosomes, essential for membrane fusion [19, 20]. If SARS-CoV-2 is internalized by receptor-mediated endocytosis and delivered to lysosomes, the virus can be prevented by CQ and HCQ that block function of the lysosome. In the presence of CQ and HCQ, SARS-CoV-2 viruses that require acidic pH to fuse with the cell membrane can no longer do so, and thus cells are protected from infection.

Several caveats associated with this data-driven study need attention. The sample size is small—only three samples from patients with moderate symptoms and six with severe symptoms were considered. These samples are imbalanced with respect to gender, age, and other covariates. Moreover, a whole set of side effects of CQ and HCQ were not assessed in this study.

4   Conclusion

In conclusion, we applied the network-based comparative analysis, implemented in our machine learning workflow scTenifoldNet, to scRNA-seq data from COVID-19 patients with different levels of severity. We found that genes of the *Malaria* pathway expressed in macrophages are significantly differentially regulated between patients with moderate and severe symptoms. Our findings help reveal the mechanisms of action of CQ and HCQ during SARS-CoV-2 infection, providing new evidence to support the use of these antimalarial drugs in the treatment of COVID-19, especially for patients who are mildly affected or in the early stage of the infection. The code and data of our study are available at https://github.com/cailab-tamu/covid19-antimalarials-letter.

References

1. Joob, B., Wiwanitkit, V.: Evidence of protective effect of hydroxychloroquine on COVID-19. J. Rheumatol. **47**, 1587–1587 (2020)
2. Romao, V.C., Cruz-Machado, A.R., Fonseca, J.E.: No evidence so far on the protective effect of hydroxychloroquine to prevent COVID-19: response to the comment by Joob and Wiwanitkit. Ann. Rheum. Dis. **80**(2), e22 (2020)
3. Gautret, P., et al.: Hydroxychloroquine and azithromycin as a treatment of COVID-19: results of an open-label non-randomized clinical trial. Int. J. Antimicrob. Agents **56**, 105949 (2020)
4. Toumi, M., Aballea, S.: Commentary on "Hydroxychloroquine and azithromycin as a treatment of COVID-19: results of an open label non-randomized clinical trial" by Gautret et al. J. Mark Access Health Policy **8**(1), 1758390 (2020)
5. Arshad, S., et al.: Treatment with Hydroxychloroquine, Azithromycin, and Combination in Patients Hospitalized with COVID-19. Int. J. Infect. Dis. **97**, 396–403 (2020)
6. Schrezenmeier, E., Dorner, T.: Mechanisms of action of hydroxychloroquine and chloroquine: implications for rheumatology. Nat. Rev. Rheumatol. **16**(3), 155–166 (2020)
7. Liu, J., et al.: Hydroxychloroquine, a less toxic derivative of chloroquine, is effective in inhibiting SARS-CoV-2 infection in vitro. Cell. Discov. **6**, 16 (2020)
8. Colson, P., et al.: Chloroquine and hydroxychloroquine as available weapons to fight COVID-19. Int. J. Antimicrob. Agents **55**(4), 105932 (2020)
9. Rolain, J.M., Colson, P., Raoult, D.: Recycling of chloroquine and its hydroxyl analogue to face bacterial, fungal and viral infections in the 21st century. Int. J. Antimicrob. Agents **30**(4), 297–308 (2007)
10. Yao, X., et al.: In vitro antiviral activity and projection of optimized dosing design of hydroxychloroquine for the treatment of severe acute respiratory syndrome coronavirus 2 (SARS-CoV-2). Clin. Infect. Dis. **71**, 732–739 (2020)
11. Wang, M., et al.: Remdesivir and chloroquine effectively inhibit the recently emerged novel coronavirus (2019-nCoV) in vitro. Cell Res. **30**(3), 269–271 (2020)

12. Gao, J., Tian, Z., Yang, X.: Breakthrough: chloroquine phosphate has shown apparent efficacy in treatment of COVID-19 associated pneumonia in clinical studies. Biosci. Trends **14**(1), 72–73 (2020)
13. Liao, M., et al.: Single-cell landscape of bronchoalveolar immune cells in patients with COVID-19. Nat. Med. **26**(6), 842–844 (2020)
14. Osorio, D., et al.: scTenifoldNet: a machine learning workflow for constructing and comparing transcriptome-wide gene regulatory networks from single-cell data. Patterns (N Y) **1**(9), 100139 (2020)
15. Dinarello, C.A.: The history of fever, leukocytic pyrogen and interleukin-1. Temperature (Austin) **2**(1), 8–16 (2015)
16. Liu, Y., et al.: Increased expression of TLR2 in CD4(+) T cells from SLE patients enhances immune reactivity and promotes IL-17 expression through histone modifications. Eur. J. Immunol. **45**(9), 2683–2693 (2015)
17. Fox, R.: Antimalarial drugs: possible mechanisms of action in autoimmune disease and prospects for drug development. Lupus **5**(Suppl 1), S4–10 (1996)
18. Gies, V., et al.: Beyond anti-viral effects of chloroquine/hydroxychloroquine. Front. Immunol. **11**, 1409 (2020)
19. Mauthe, M., et al.: Chloroquine inhibits autophagic flux by decreasing autophagosome-lysosome fusion. Autophagy **14**(8), 1435–1455 (2018)
20. Savarino, A., et al.: Effects of chloroquine on viral infections: an old drug against today's diseases? Lancet Infect. Dis. **3**(11), 722–727 (2003)

Computational Advances for Next Generation Sequencing

RACCROCHE: Ancestral Flowering Plant Chromosomes and Gene Orders Based on Generalized Adjacencies and Chromosomal Gene Co-occurrences

Qiaoji Xu[1], Lingling Jin[2], Chunfang Zheng[1], James H. Leebens Mack[3], and David Sankoff[1(✉)]

[1] University of Ottawa, Ottawa, ON K1N 6N5, Canada
{qxu062,sankoff}@uottawa.ca
[2] University of Saskatchewan, Saskatoon, SK S7N 5C9, Canada
lingling.jin@cs.usask.ca
[3] University of Georgia, Athens, GA 30602, USA
jleebensmack@uga.edu

Abstract. Given the phylogenetic relationships of several extant species, the reconstruction of their ancestral genomes at the gene and chromosome level is made difficult by the cycles of whole genome doubling followed by fractionation in plant lineages. Fractionation scrambles the gene adjacencies that enable existing reconstruction methods. We propose an alternative approach that postpones the selection of gene adjacencies for reconstructing small ancestral segments and instead accumulates a very large number of syntenically validated candidate adjacencies to produce long ancestral contigs through maximum weight matching. Likewise, we do not construct chromosomes by successively piecing together contigs into larger segments, but instead count all contig co-occurrences on the input genomes and cluster these, so that chromosomal assemblies of contigs all emerge naturally ordered at each ancestral node of the phylogeny. These strategies result in substantially more complete reconstructions than existing methods. We deploy a number of quality measures: contig lengths, continuity of contig structure on successive ancestors, coverage of the reconstruction on the input genomes, and rearrangement implications of the chromosomal structures obtained. The reconstructed ancestors can be functionally annotated and are visualized by painting the ancestral projections on the descendant genomes, and by highlighting syntenic ancestor-descendant relationships. We apply our methods to genomes drawn from a broad range of monocot orders, confirming the tetraploidization event "tau" in the stem lineage between the alismatids and the lilioids.

Keywords: Genome reconstruction · Gene order · Polyploidization · Fractionation · Monocots · Generalized adjacencies · Multiple orthology · Safe phylogeny · Maximum weight matching · Co-occurrence matrix · Complete-link clustering · Linear ordering problem

© Springer Nature Switzerland AG 2021
S. K. Jha et al. (Eds.): ICCABS 2020, LNBI 12686, pp. 97–115, 2021.
https://doi.org/10.1007/978-3-030-79290-9_9

1   Introduction

Reconstruction methods depending on conserved gene adjacencies tend to break down in plants, largely because the history of whole genome doubling and tripling events (WGD and WGT, respectively) in the lineages of plants. All known flowering plant genomes (except *Amborella trichopoda* [1]) have at least one, and often several, WGDs or WGTs in their lineages since the ancestral angiosperm, followed by extensive loss of redundant genes, largely randomly distributed along one or other of the duplicated chromosomes. These processes effectively scramble gene order and disrupt most adjacencies. Subsequently, most of the sets of duplicate or triplicate genes created by WGD/WGT events are reduced sooner or later to a single gene, by the redundance-eliminating process known as gene fractionation. Because of this fractionation, duplication of a genome fragment containing genes in the order 1-2-3-4-5-6, for example, may result in two surviving orders 1-3-5 and 2-4-6, with none of the five fragment-internal adjacencies conserved, and only one adjacency at most conserved with the chromosomal regions surrounding each copy of the fragment. The situation is compounded if there are several WGD or WGT events in the history of some of the present-day genomes. All this is superimposed on a background of gene family expansion through tandem duplication or other mechanisms, and loss of genes from species for which they are no longer physiologically or ecologically essential, genome rearrangement and other processes, all of which disrupt adjacencies independently of the fractionation process.

For this paper, we developed a pipeline for ancestral plant genome inference, RACCROCHE, **R**econstruction of **AnC**estral **CO**ntigs and **CH**romosom**E**s, including some intermediate ancestral genomes giving rise to major plant subgroupings. The new strategy implemented in our approach combines six fundamental components:

1. The replacement of the traditional selection of 1-1 orthologs among input genomes, as a first step, by the identification of many-to-many correspondences among gene families of limited size within these genomes.
2. The use of generalized adjacencies [17,18], namely any pair of genes close to each other on a chromosome, instead of just immediately adjacent genes.

These first two components avoid premature decisions on which orthologies and which adjacencies should be incorporated in the final reconstruction, in contrast to approaches which insist on making these decisions early in the reconstruction process, e.g., [11].

3. The compilation of oriented candidate adjacencies at each of the ancestral nodes of a given binary branching tree phylogeny using a "safe" criterion - that such an adjacency must be evidenced in genomes in two or three of the subtrees connected by this node, not just one or none.
4. The large set of these candidates is then resolved, at each node, by maximum weight matching (MWM) to give an optimally compatible subset, which ipso

facto defines linearly (or circularly) compatible "contigs" of the ancestral genomes to be constructed, thus avoiding the branching segments that plague other methods [14].

5. A local sequence matching, satisfying proximity and contiguity conditions, of each contig on all of the chromosomes of the input genomes. This step includes the construction of a total chromosomal co-occurrence matrix of contigs belonging to each ancestral node.

6. A clustering applied to the co-occurrence matrix. This is then decomposed into chromosomal sets of contigs, with the aid of a heat map comparison of the contigs as organized by the clustering. Within each contig, the order of the genes is already predetermined by the MWM step. Ordering the contigs along the chromosomes is carried out by a linear ordering algorithm. The assignment and ordering of contigs to construct entire chromosomes, and not just a collection of small regions, is an advance over previous methods. Corresponding chromosomes in different ancestral genomes can be identified by the similar contigs they contain.

The results of this pipeline are mapped back to the input genomes, indicating how these extant genomes were derived through chromosomal rearrangements from their immediate ancestral genome.

We provide an evaluation of the reconstruction in terms of the sizes of the ancient chromosomal fragments found, the coherence (or continuity) between adjacent ancestral genomes, the coverage of the ancestors when mapped to extant genomes, and the "choppiness" of this mapping in terms of ancestor-descendant rearrangement.

There has been much recent work on the reconstruction of ancestral plant genomes [3, 4, 10, 12, 19]; on the computational side most of this has been based on common gene adjacencies in extant genomes, as summarized in such structures as sets of species trees and contiguous ancestral regions (CARS) [2]. The latter terminology, introduced successfully in the context of mammalian genomes [7], where there are no polyploidizations since the common ancestor, and then taken over to plant genomics [4, 5, 12], applies to a series of methods of which a recent improved exemplar is proCARs [11]. We will show that in the case of flowering plants, the avoidance of premature selection of gene adjacencies in RACCROCHE allows the recovery of more of the ancestral genome than proCARs.

The rest of the paper is organized as follows. Section 2 presents the features and procedure of the algorithm. (Most of the details appear in appendices.) An application of the RACCROCHE pipeline is shown in Sect. 3 with a focus on the reconstruction of the four monocot ancestors in the known phylogeny relating six extant monocot plant genomes. These include *Acorus calamus* (sweet flag) from the order Acorales, *Spirodela polyrhiza* (duckweed) from the order Alismatales, *Dioscorea rotundata* (yam) from the order Dioscorales, *Asparagus officinalis* (asparagus) from the order Aspargales, *Elaeis guineensis* (African oil palm) from the order Arecales and *Ananas comosus* (pineapple) from the order Poales. This includes an evaluation of the reconstruction in terms of the sizes of the ancient chromosomal fragments found, the coherence between adjacent ancestral genomes, the coverage of the ancestors when mapped to extant genomes, and the "choppiness" of this mapping in terms of ancestry descendant rearrangement. Section 4 concludes the paper and outlines some future directions.

2   Methods

2.1   Input

The input to RACCROCHE consists of N annotated extant genomes related by a given unrooted binary branching phylogeny, and a number of parameters, including

W: window size to include generalized as well as immediate adjacencies,
NF: largest total gene family size allowed in ortholog grouping in all extant genomes,
NG: largest gene family size allowed in any one genome,
NC: the number of longest contigs in ancestral genomes to be matched to extant genomes,
K: the desired number of chromosomes for each ancestor,
DIS: the maximum distance between two adjacent genes in an extant genome to be matched with adjacent genes in an ancestral contig.

Figure 1 depicts the overall flow of the RACCROCHE pipeline.

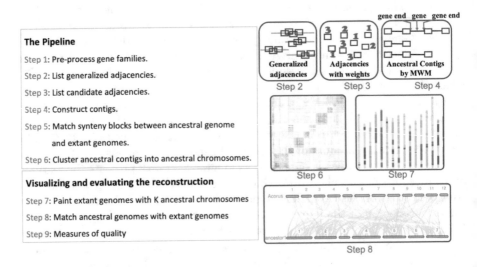

Fig. 1. Overall flow of the RACCROCHE procedure.

2.2   The Pipeline

Step 1: Pre-process gene families. Pre-processing for the RACCROCHE procedure starts with syntenically validated orthogroups, or gene families, constructed from $\frac{1}{2}(N^2 + N)$ between-genome and self-comparison sets of pairwise SynMap synteny blocks by accumulating all genes that are syntenically orthologous to at least one other gene in the family. It retains only those families with at most a preset number NF of members and at most NG members in any particular genome. Without loss of generality, $NF \leq N \times NG$.

The use of syntenically validated adjacencies only, restricted to genes appearing in synteny blocks identified by the comparison of some pair of the descendant genomes, avoids generating huge gene families and astronomical numbers of adjacencies not reflective of the ancestor.

An optional second "redistribution" step for genes in large families is described in Appendix A.

Step 2: List generalized adjacencies. For each of the N extant genomes, RACCROCHE compiles all generalized adjacencies, i.e., representatives of two gene families, occurring within a window of a preset size, W, in the order of genes on a chromosome. The adjacencies are oriented by the DNA strand or strands containing the two genes, so that we can distinguish the two ends of each gene and identify which ends are involved in the adjacency.

Step 3: List candidate adjacencies. For each ancestral tree node, allow only adjacencies in occurring in two or three of the three subtrees connected by a branch incident to that node as candidates to be adjacencies in the corresponding ancestral genome. Occurrence in a subtree means occurrence in at least one of the extant genomes in that subtree.

Step 4: Construct contigs. With candidate adjacencies weighted 2 or 3 according to whether they occur in 2 or 3 subtrees, use maximum weight matching to extract the highest weight set of compatible adjacencies, i.e., each gene end is matched to at most one other gene end, which automatically defines a set of disjoint linear contigs for the ancestral genome.

A method for improving the coherence of successive ancestors is discussed in Appendix B. This comes at the cost of other qualities of the contigs, and will not be discussed further here.

Step 5: Match synteny blocks between ancestral genome and extant genomes. For each of the NC longest contigs of an ancestral genome, search for locally matched regions - synteny blocks - in all N extant genomes. This process is formally described in Appendix C.

Step 6: Cluster ancestral contigs into ancestral chromosomes. Clustering of ancestral chromosomes is based on co-occurrence of ancestral contigs of sufficient size on the same chromosomes of extant genomes. First, a co-occurrence matrix is constructed on the set of contigs counting the cumulative number of times two different contigs are matched on the same chromosome in one or more extant genomes. Next, a complete-link clustering of the contigs is performed in each ancestral genome, based on the co-occurrence matrix. The hierarchical cluster thus produced is decomposed either automatically (e.g., with a cut-off level or with a cluster size criterion) or with some biologically-motivated manual intervention into a preset number K of chromosomes. See Sect. 3.2 below for an example.

Contigs are ordered by applying the algorithm of linear ordering problem [13] based on the count of relative ordering, the number of times each contig appears upstream/downstream of the other contig for every pair of contigs within a cluster.

The clustering and ordering are detailed in Appendix D. These procedures have been validated through simulation studies [16].

2.3   Visualizing and Evaluating the Reconstruction

Step 7: Painting the extant genomes according to the ancestral chromosomes. Each of the K chromosomes of an ancestor genome is assigned a different colour. Each extant genome can then be painted by the colours of an ancestor based on the coordinates of synteny blocks calculated in Step 5. Unpainted regions less than 1Mb long between two blocks of the same colour are also painted with that colour. Although we can establish a general correspondence between the chromosomes of the successive ancestor genomes, the synteny blocks and the painting of the extant genomes will nevertheless depend on which ancestor is used. Generally the immediate ancestor of a genome gives the most meaningful painting.

Step 8: Adapting MCScanX to match ancestral genomes with extant genomes. We use MCScanX [15] to connect matching parts of each descendant and its immediate ancestor, as well as to calculate the optimal order of chromosomes.

MCScanX requires both gene location and gene sequence to search pairwise synteny. The "genes" in the constructed ancestors, however, are really gene familes, each represented by an integer label. For the purposes of MCScanX, we simply choose a member of the gene family, either randomly, or from a descendant of that ancestor.

For viewing purposes, the number of "crossing" lines in the trace diagram should be minimized. MCScanX searches for the ordering of the chromosomes that minimizes this, using a genetic algorithm.

Step 9: Measures of Quality. In the construction of the contigs, we count how many gene families and how many candidate adjacencies are incorporated in total by the MWM and in the longest NC chromosomes. We also document details of the *contig length distribution*, e.g., the longest contig and N50.

The *coherence* between all pairs of contig sets, each set associated with one ancestor is a way of more global way of assessing the reconstruction. To be credible, the contigs at one ancestral node should resemble to some extent the contigs at a neighbouring ancestor.

A measure of commonality between two contigs i and j from two ancestors I and J respectively, is given by

$$\text{sim}_{ij} = \frac{x_{ij}}{\sqrt{x_{i.} x_{.j}}}, \qquad (1)$$

where $x_{i.}, x_{.j}$ and x_{ij} are the numbers of gene families in contig i, in contig j and in both contigs, respectively.

Then, calculating the coherence between two tree nodes for the NC longest contigs.

$$\text{coherence}_{IJ} = \frac{\sum_i \max_{j=1}^{NC} \text{sim}_{ij}}{NC}. \qquad (2)$$

Percent coverage is defined as the percentage that genome G is covered by the synteny block set of ancestor A. It also reflects how closely ancestor A is related to G.

Choppiness of painting in G is quantitatively measured by the number of different colours, T, the number of single-colour regions, R, and the number of small stripes, X, on each extant chromosome [9]. T is defined as the sum number of different colours on each chromosome of G minus 1, reflecting how much inter-chromosomal exchange, such as translocation, there has been; R is defined as the sum number of single-colour regions on each chromosome of G and is a measure of how much intra-chromosomal movement (e.g., reversals or transpositions) there has been; X is defined as the number of stripes less than a certain threshold size (i.e. 300 Kbp), which we deduct to avoid inflating R. The choppiness measure of painting in G is written as $R - X$.

2.4   Ancestral Gene Function

To aid in future studies of the genomic organization of gene function, a GO-term enrichment analysis of the members of each gene family is implemented to produce a functional annotation for the inferred ancestral genes. The details are reported in Appendix E, but are not applied in this paper.

3   Reconstruction of Monocot Ancestors

We applied our method to the reconstruction of four monocot ancestors, given six extant monocot plant genomes from *Acorus calamus* (sweet flag), *Spirodela polyrhiza* (duckweed), *Dioscorea rotundata* (yam), *Asparagus officinalis* (asparagus), *Elaeis guineensis* (African oil palm) and *Ananas comosus* (pineapple). The phylogenetic tree is shown in Fig. 2. The divergence time from Ancestor 1 to any of the extant genomes is about 130 Mya [6]. The reconstruction problem is difficult due not only to this lengthy elapsed time, since the early Cretaceous, comparable to that of the early divergence of placental mammals, but also to the occurrence of at least one WGD in every order, and generally two or more.

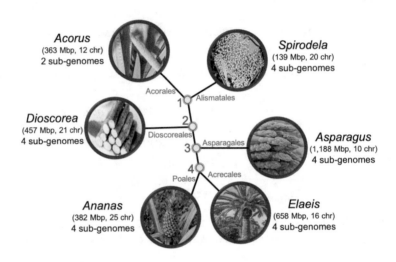

Fig. 2. Phylogeny showing relationships among six monocots and their ancestors.

One question we aimed to answer was whether both ancient WGD detected in the extant *Dioscorea* genome occurred after its branching off the stem lineage to Asparagales, Arecales and Poales, or whether one of these WGD occurred earlier, between Ancestors 1 and 2, and is identical to the "tau" event known to affect all these later branching orders.

3.1   Properties of the Contig Reconstruction

After numerous trials, input parameters that seemed (somewhat subjectively) to balance contig length properties, coherence and coverage were chosen to be window size $W = 7$, maximum total family size $NF = 50$ and within-genome maximum family size $NG = 10$. Table 1 summarizes the gene content of each of the input genomes, first, syntenically validated genes (i.e., in synteny blocks); second, after removing very large gene families; third, after filtering for within-genome family size; fourth, genes present in a candidate adjacency; fifth, genes incorporated in the 250 longest contigs for any ancestor.

Table 1. Numbers of genes at each step of building contigs.

	In synteny blocks	In families <5000	In filtered families	In candidate adjacencies	In contigs, after MWM
Acorus	21,308	11,807	11,300	10,189	9,649
Spirodela	20,751	8,385	8,005	7,706	7,276
Dioscorea	19,240	8,256	7,873	7,485	7,141
Asparagus	28,141	10,109	9,645	9,128	8,750
Ananas	27,024	11,744	11,180	10,623	10,116
Elaeis	21,425	12,833	12,227	11,831	11,369

Recall that to be a candidate, an adjacency must appear at least once in at least two different genomes, thus satisfying the safety criterion for at least one ancestor. Applying the MWM algorithm to the set of candidates greatly reduces the number in selecting the best linearized subset, as documented in Table 2.

Table 2. Input adjacencies to MWM, and output.

	Ancestor 1	Ancestor 2	Ancestor 3	Ancestor 4
Candidate adjacencies	35,165	41,963	47,118	48,452
MWM adjacencies	6,335	6,847	7,244	7,310

The contigs that are formed by the MWM matches are of moderate length, as suggested by Table 3. The longest one contains 84–89 genes and the last one retained ($NC = 250$) contains around 10 genes. We then locate all the matches of these contigs on the chromosomes of the extant genomes.

A good proportion of the MWM adjacencies will be shared by successive (or all) ancestors, and many contigs will be similar from ancestor to ancestor. Table 4 displays the coherence among the contig sets for the four ancestor genomes.

Table 3. Contig statistics for the four ancestors. The number of genes in a contig measures its length.

	Longest contig	Total number of contigs	N50		N60		N70	
			Length	Number	Length	Number	Length	Number
Ancestor 1	84	3,950	10	249	5	403	1	662
Ancestor 2	89	3,441	12	219	8	292	3	510
Ancestor 3	85	3,043	15	169	10	252	5	393
Ancestor 4	88	2,975	17	151	12	215	6	342

Table 4. Coherence among ancestors.

	Ancestor 1	Ancestor 2	Ancestor 3	Ancestor 4
Ancestor 1	1.000			
Ancestor 2	0.430	1.000		
Ancestor 3	0.361	0.443	1.000	
Ancestor 4	0.318	0.357	0.419	1.000

Table 5. Contigs and genes in ancestral chromosomes.

Chromosome	Ancestor 1		Ancestor 2		Ancestor 3		Ancestor 4	
	Contigs	Genes	Contigs	Genes	Contigs	Genes	Contigs	Genes
1	43	857	42	1,398	40	1,909	44	1,911
2	40	729	43	585	43	683	46	703
3	23	363	21	443	22	467	18	620
4	44	951	39	671	42	853	38	917
5	41	773	43	894	32	656	40	810
6	23	536	23	666	30	958	31	985
7	36	743	39	844	41	497	33	411
Total	250	4,952	250	5,501	250	6,013	250	6,357

3.2   Clustering

The choice of complete link method of hierarchical clustering is appropriate in the context of searching for balanced clusters at all levels, and avoiding an asymmetric "chaining" effect. Chromosomes in a genome tend to be roughly the same order of magnitude, which therefore suggests complete link.

The hierarchical cluster of the 250 longest contigs according to their chromosomal co-occurrence (Sect. 2.2) is seen beside each panel in Fig. 3. The intensity of the shading of each cell in the heat map reflects how frequently the corresponding contigs co-occur in the extant genomes. In each case seven large, darkly shaded, blocks emerge neatly from the map, thus constituting the chromosomes of the ancestral genome. Table 5 contains statistics on the chromosomes and contigs.

3.3   Painting the Chromosomes of the Present-Day Genomes

Each chromosome in an ancestor genome is assigned a colour. Despite the genome rearrangements intervening between an earlier ancestor and a later one, corresponding chromosomes in different ancestral genomes can be identified by similarity in the gene content of their constituent contigs. This correspondence, though it disrupted in many places by interchromosomal exchanges, is reflected in the chromosomal colour assignment in the four ancestors. The colours are then projected onto the chromosomes of the extant genomes that served as inputs to

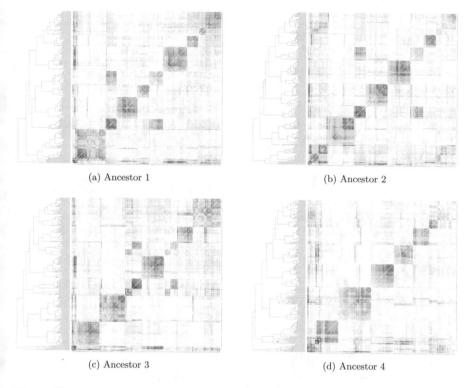

(a) Ancestor 1   (b) Ancestor 2

(c) Ancestor 3   (d) Ancestor 4

Fig. 3. Heat maps of the four ancestors showing the clusters of contigs making up ancestral chromosomes from the longest 250 contigs by the complete-link clustering algorithm.

the pipeline, based on the contig matches detected in Sect. 3.1. Painting is carried out as described in Sect. 2.3 and is depicted in Fig. 4.

3.4 Evaluation

Tables 6 and 7 provide quality assessments of the reconstruction as manifest in the painted extant genomes. In Table 6 we see a high degree of coverage of the extant genomes, while Table 7 shows a degree of choppiness that is moderate, given the time scale involved. Ancestors 1 and 2 achieve better coverage of all the extant genomes, even though most of the genomes were more directly involved in the reconstruction of Ancestors 3 and 4. This may be an artifact of the sparsity of matches from Ancestors 1 and 2, so that the inter-block colouring discussed in Sect. 2.3 can cover longer, uninterrupted, regions of the chromosomes. A similar sparsity explanation can also be entertained for the low degree of choppiness of the paintings on the *Spirodela* genome, despite its higher degree of polyploidy than *Acorus*.

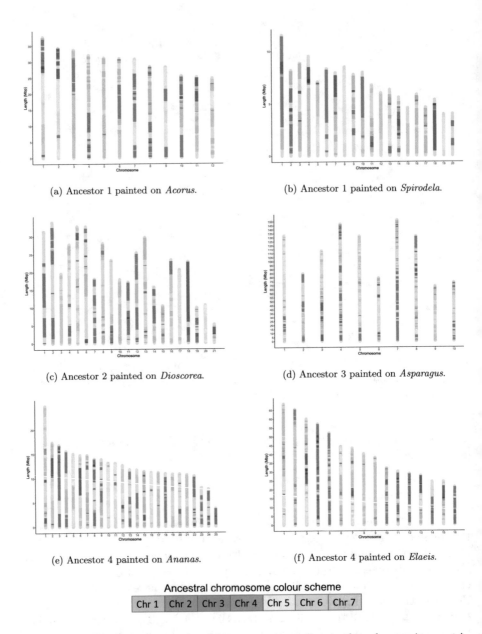

(a) Ancestor 1 painted on *Acorus*.

(b) Ancestor 1 painted on *Spirodela*.

(c) Ancestor 2 painted on *Dioscorea*.

(d) Ancestor 3 painted on *Asparagus*.

(e) Ancestor 4 painted on *Ananas*.

(f) Ancestor 4 painted on *Elaeis*.

Ancestral chromosome colour scheme

| Chr 1 | Chr 2 | Chr 3 | Chr 4 | Chr 5 | Chr 6 | Chr 7 |

Fig. 4. Chromosome painting of extant genomes according to the colour assignment in their immediate ancestors. Ancestral blocks shorter than 150 Kbp are not shown.

Table 6. Percent coverage of extant genomes by ancestral chromosomes.

	Ancestor 1	Ancestor 2	Ancestor 3	Ancestor 4
Acorus	81%	80%	82%	83%
Spirodela	74%	78%	80%	81%
Dioscorea	54%	61%	62%	63%
Asparagus	63%	62%	66%	71%
Ananas	62%	69%	71%	70%
Elaeis	75%	79%	83%	84%

Table 7. Choppiness of painting on extant genomes. T reflects how much inter-chromosomal exchange has occurred, $R - T$ is a measure of intra-chromosomal movement (e.g., reversals or transpositions) and X is the number of small stripes shorter than 300 Kbp, which misleadingly inflates R.

T	*Acorus*	*Spirodela*	*Dioscorea*	*Asparagus*	*Ananas*	*Elaeis*
Ancestor 1	45	33	48	40	48	59
Ancestor 2	38	22	45	38	38	57
Ancestor 3	48	36	48	43	42	60
Ancestor 4	50	39	57	47	55	65
$R - T$	*Acorus*	*Spirodela*	*Dioscorea*	*Asparagus*	*Ananas*	*Elaeis*
Ancestor 1	122	56	128	233	88	193
Ancestor 2	95	34	107	220	94	161
Ancestor 3	129	51	131	284	104	194
Ancestor 4	172	75	140	331	124	247
$R - X$	*Acorus*	*Spirodela*	*Dioscorea*	*Asparagus*	*Ananas*	*Elaeis*
Ancestor 1	134	63	136	239	106	216
Ancestor 2	112	45	121	221	100	196
Ancestor 3	142	64	143	283	110	215
Ancestor 4	170	74	166	337	137	270

3.5   MCScanX Visualization

A different view of the evolution of the monocot genomes via ancestral intermediates is obtained through connecting homologous synteny blocks in a MCScanX visualization, as laid out in Fig. 5. Consistent with the history of extensive rearrangement evident in Fig. 4 and Table 7, the patterns of MCScanX connections is rather complex. Nevertheless, we can find important relationships using the "highlight" feature of the software.

Thus, the comparison between Ancestor 1 and *Acorus* shows several chromosomal regions in the ancestor each linked to two regions in the extant genome, whereas the opposite pattern is non-existent. Similarly the comparison between Ancestor 1 and *Spirodela* also shows instances of a 1:4 pattern, consistent with the two WGDs inherited by this species.

The most interesting pattern, however, is that between Ancestors 1 and 2, which strongly suggests a duplication event occurring before the branching of the *Dioscorales* from the main monocot stem lineage. In contrast the Ancestor 2-Ancestor 3 and Ancestor 3-Ancestor 4 comparisons both show 1-1 patterns. Moreover, though dot-plot examination of *Dioscorea* evidences four subgenomes, thus two WGD in its history, the MCScanX diagram of Ancestor 2-*Dioscorea* only shows evidence of one event, confirming that one event must have predated Ancestor 2. This latter event is the one shared by all the more recently branching orders, known as "tau".

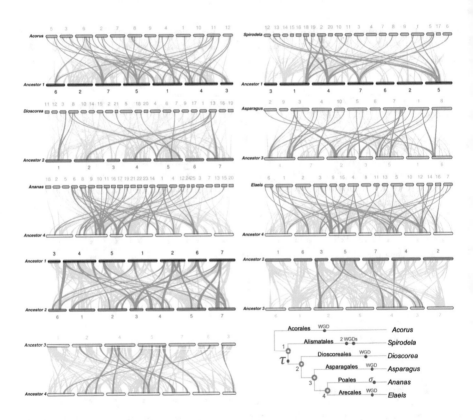

Fig. 5. Matching genomes, extant and ancestral, with their immediate ancestors.

4   Discussions and Conclusions

This work explored an alternative approach to genome reconstruction by stepwise piecing together of small units. Instead, we compile a large number of potential components and use a combinatorial optimization approach to combining them, an approach explicitly disavowed by, e.g., [11]. We were motivated by the special case of plant comparative genomics, which has to deal with the aftermath or recurrent polyploidization and fractionation. Compared to approaches like `proCARs` [11] which is very successful in reconstructing ancestral animal genomes, `RACCROCHE` may work better with plant genomes, since it is designed to be robust against the gene order scrambling effect of fractionation.

Since the entities reconstructed by `proCARs` are not meant to be individual ancestral genes, but blocks of syntenically related genes identified at the level of extant genomes, it is hard to compare our inferred ancestral genomes, composed of hypothetical genes with identifiable functions, with the output of `proCARs`. In our hands `proCARs` identified 214 synteny blocks in our data, organized into "CARs" (contiguous ancestral regions) making up the ancestral genomes. These contained a total of 3,248 "universal seeds", which may be comparable to our ancestral genes, although our ancestors contained about twice as many. Insofar as these comparisons are valid, they confirm a role for `RACCROCHE` in plant comparative genomics.

One particular feature that stands out in this work, is the innovative clustering of counts of contig co-occurrences on extant chromosomes, followed by heatmap construction to identify ancestral chromosomes. Another is the use of MCScanX to locate a WGD on an internal branch of a phylogeny.

Acknowledgements. We thank the Department of Energy Joint Genome Institute staff and collaborators including David Kudrna, Jerry Jenkins, Jane Grimwood, Shengqiang Shu, and Jeremy Schmutz for pre-publication access to the *Acorus* genome sequence and annotation. Thanks to Aîda Ouangraoua for much help in implementing ProCARs [11] and Haibao Tang for prompt replies to queries about MCScanX [15].

Funding. Research supported by Discovery grants to LJ and DS from the Natural Sciences and Engineering Research Council of Canada. DS holds the Canada Research Chair in Mathematical Genomics.

Availability. The annotated genomic data is accessible on the `CoGe` platform https://genomevolution.org/coge/ and Phytozome. The pipeline is available at https://github.com/jin-repo/RACCROCHE.

Appendices

A   Redistributing Genes from Families Exceeding Upper Size Limits

As an optional second "redistribution" step, all families with more than NF members or more than NG members in any particular genome, are flagged. Then the construction of the families is repeated, with the restriction that no gene can be recruited to a family by virtue only of a similarity of less than some threshold homology level θ to a gene already in the family. The intent is to break up large families held together by a few weak links, and thus to retrieve some better supported smaller families.

B   Modes of Contig Construction

RACCROCHE executes for a single set of W, NF, NG parameters, or for a range of values of W and NG. In the latter case, there is an option, designed to increase coherence among sets of contigs for successive ancestors, that the MWM for any combination of W and NG must be restricted to include all adjacencies already recovered for lesser values of W or NG, insofar as possible. Thus, starting with some small W and NG, we can construct MWM solutions for larger window size and/or larger gene family size, and hence sets of contigs, by incrementing one or the other of the parameters.

It is possible, however, to have conflicts between $W, NG - 1$, and $W - 1, NG$ analyses. For example if adjacencies (a, b) and (b, c) are in the MWM for $(W, NG - 1)$ and (a, b) and (b, d) are in the MWM for $(W - 1, NG)$, then a matching for W, G cannot be forced to include all matchings from the two previous MWM. To accommodate this possibility, when we restrict the MWM for (W, NG) to include all adjacencies from $(W, NG - 1)$ and $(W - 1, NG)$, we make an exception for any adjacencies from either that are in potential conflict with adjacencies from the other. Thus (a, b) in the example above might be obligatorily included, but (b, c) and (b, d) would not. Thus the MWM for (W, NG) might include (b, c) or (b, d), but not both.

C   Matching Contigs to Chromosomes of Extant Genomes

For the ancestor genome, A, computed from a set of extant genomes neighbouring A, $G_{1 \cdots n}$, perform the following steps.

1. Extract gene features of ancestor A in descendant genomes.
   For every gene, g, in ancestor A computed from Step 2, retrieve six features of this gene in every extant genome $G_{1 \cdots n}$ involved in constructing ancestor A. The features of a gene include chromosome ID, start and end chromosomal positions, distance between g to its next adjacent gene in G_i, gene family ID labelled in Step 1, and contig ID in A, denoted as $g^{A \to G_i}(chr, start, end, distance, gf, ctg)$.

2. Map ancestor A to each of the descendant genomes.
   The ancestor will be mapped as ancestral syntenic blocks on the descendant genome in two steps. The first step initializes a syntenic block by merging two adjacent genes given a distance threshold DIS: merge two genes, g_1 and g_2, forming one ancestral syntenic block on G_i if g_1 and g_2 satisfy the following conditions:

   (a) g_1 and g_2 locate the same chromosome of G_i;
   (b) g_1 and g_2 are adjacent to each other; in other words, there could be a non-coding region but no other gene(s) between g_1 and g_2;
   (c) The distance between the two adjacent genes must be less than or equal to the distance threshold DIS (i.e. $DIS = 1 \, \text{Mbp}$).

The second step extends the above identified ancestral syntenic block by merging flanking gene(s) into the block if the gene(s) satisfies the above three conditions. It stops extending the block if no flanking gene could be merged into the block. After the two steps, an ancestral synteny block mapping A to G_i is denoted as $syntenyBlk(chr, start, end, ctg, len)$. The set of synteny blocks between A and G_i is

$syntenyBlkSet^{A \to G_i} = \{syntenyBlk_k(chr, start, end, ctg, len) | 1 \leq k \leq m,$
where m is the total number of synteny blocks mapping from A to $G_i\}$

D   Construction of Ancestral Chromosomes

1. Filter the set of blocks longer than a block length threshold.
   Given a block length threshold, $blockLEN$, $\overline{syntenyBlkSet}^{A \to G_i}$ is a subset of $syntenyBlkSet^{A \to G_i}$, where each block in the set is longer than $blockLEN$ (i.e. $blockLEN = 150$ Kbp).
2. Count co-occurrence of ancestral contigs on same chromosomes.
   Based on $syntenyBlk.chr$ and $syntenyBlk.ctg$ of each pair of synteny block in $\overline{syntenyBlkSet}^{A \to G_i}$, gather the co-occurrence of ancestral contigs on the same extant chromosome. Write the co-occurrence result into the lower triangle of a $NC \times NC$ matrix, m, where the rows and columns are contigs with ID from 0 to $(NC - 1)$, $m_{i,j}$ is the number of co-occurrence between contigs i and j, where $0 < j < i < NC - 1$. The maximum co-occurrence frequency in m is denoted as $\max_{freq}$.
3. Cluster ancestral contigs into ancestral chromosomes according to pairwise distance matrix based on co-occurrence.
   A NC by NC distance matrix, $dmat$, is calculated as

$$dmat_{i,j} = -\log(\frac{\max_{freq} - m_{i,j}}{\max_{freq}}).$$

This distance matrix is fed into the complete-link clustering algorithm. This can then be composed into K clusters, according to users' preferences. The resultant clusters of contigs correspond to ancestral chromosomes and their compositions.

Last, attach ancestral chromosome number as an attribute to each of the synteny block:

$$syntenyBlkSet^{A \to G_{1 \cdots N}} = \{syntenyBlk_k(chr, start, end, ctg, len, ancestral_{chr})\},$$

where $ancestral\_chr$ corresponds to the cluster ID which blk.ctg belong to.
To order the contigs along each chromosome, we proceed as follows.
After the $syntenyBlkSet^{A \to G_{1 \cdots N}}$ is generated in Step 3, relative ordering between every pair of contigs is counted. The number of times each contig appears upstream/downstream of other contig is structured into an $NC \times NC$ ordering matrix, C, where the rows and columns are contig IDs from 0 to $NC-1$.

$c_{i,j}$ represents the number of times contig i occurred in upstream of contig j in the extant chromosomes.

Given the ordering matrix C, the *linear ordering problem (LOP)* is the problem of finding a permutation π of the column and row indices $\{1, \cdots, NC\}$, such that the value

$$f(\pi) = \sum_{i=1}^{NC} \sum_{j=i+1}^{NC} C^{(\pi(i), \pi(j))} \tag{3}$$

is maximized [13]. In other words, the goal is to find a permutation of the columns and rows of C such that the sum of the elements in the upper triangle is maximized.

By applying a meta-heuristic solver of LOP, Tabu Search [8], the solution order corresponds to the ordering/permutation of contigs sorted by their positions along ancestral chromosomes.

E   Functional Annotation of Ancestral Genes

We create a set of all genes in all families represented by ancestral genes in the reconstructed ancestor. This is the background set. For each gene family, all the genes in the family constitute a query set for GO-term enrichment analysis against the background set. Significant terms that emerge constitute the functional annotation for the ancestral gene.

References

1. Amborella Genome Project: The Amborella genome and the evolution of flowering plants. Science **342**(6165), 1241089 (2013)
2. Anselmetti, Y., Luhmann, N., Bérard, S., Tannier, E., Chauve, C.: Comparative methods for reconstructing ancient genome organization. In: Setubal, J.C., Stoye, J., Stadler, P.F. (eds.) Comparative Genomics. MMB, vol. 1704, pp. 343–362. Springer, New York (2018). https://doi.org/10.1007/978-1-4939-7463-4_13
3. Avdeyev, P., Alexeev, N., Rong, Y., Alekseyev, M.A.: A unified ILP framework for core ancestral genome reconstruction problems. Bioinformatics **36**(10), 2993–3003 (2020)
4. Badouin, H., et al.: The sunflower genome provides insights into oil metabolism, flowering and Asterid evolution. Nature **546**(7656), 148–152 (2017)
5. Chauve, C., Tannier, E.: A methodological framework for the reconstruction of contiguous regions of ancestral genomes and its application to mammalian genomes. PLoS Comput. Biol. **4**(11), e1000234 (2008)
6. Givnish, T.J., et al.: Monocot plastid phylogenomics, timeline, net rates of species diversification, the power of multi-gene analyses, and a functional model for the origin of monocots. Am. J. Bot. **105**(11), 1888–1910 (2018)
7. Ma, J., et al.: Reconstructing contiguous regions of an ancestral genome. Genome Res. **16**(12), 1557–1565 (2006)
8. Martí, R., Reinelt, G., Duarte, A.: A benchmark library and a comparison of heuristic methods for the linear ordering problem. Comput. Optim. Appl. **51**(3), 1297–1317 (2012). https://doi.org/10.1007/s10589-010-9384-9

9. Mazowita, M., Haque, L., Sankoff, D.: Stability of rearrangement measures in the comparison of genome sequences. J. Comput. Biol. **13**(2), 554–566 (2006)

10. Murat, F., Armero, A., Pont, C., Klopp, C., Salse, J.: Reconstructing the genome of the most recent common ancestor of flowering plants. Nat. Genet. **49**, 490–496 (2017)

11. Perrin, A., Varré, J.S., Blanquart, S., Ouangraoua, A.: ProCARs: progressive reconstruction of ancestral gene orders. BMC Genomics **16**(S5) (2015). Article number: S6. https://doi.org/10.1186/1471-2164-16-S5-S6

12. Rubert, D.P., Martinez, F.V., Stoye, J., Doerr, D.: Analysis of local genome rearrangement improves resolution of ancestral genomic maps in plants. BMC Genomics **21**, 1–11 (2020). https://doi.org/10.1186/s12864-020-6609-x

13. Schiavinotto, T., Stützle, T.: The linear ordering problem: instances, search space analysis and algorithms. J. Math. Model. Algorithms **3**(4), 367–402 (2004). https://doi.org/10.1007/s10852-005-2583-1

14. Tannier, E., Bazin, A., Davín, A., Guéguen, L., Bérard, S., Chauve, C.: Ancestral genome organization as a diagnosis tool for phylogenomics (2020)

15. Wang, Y., et al.: MCScanX: a toolkit for detection and evolutionary analysis of gene synteny and collinearity. Nucleic Acids Res. **40**(7), e49 (2012)

16. Xu, Q., Jin, L., Zheng, C., Leebens-Mack, J.H., Sankoff, D.: Validation of automated chromosome recovery in the reconstruction of ancestral gene order. Algorithms **14**, 160 (2021)

17. Xu, X., Sankoff, D.: Tests for gene clusters satisfying the generalized adjacency criterion. In: Bazzan, A.L.C., Craven, M., Martins, N.F. (eds.) BSB 2008. LNCS, vol. 5167, pp. 152–160. Springer, Heidelberg (2008). https://doi.org/10.1007/978-3-540-85557-6_14

18. Yang, Z., Sankoff, D.: Natural parameter values for generalized gene adjacency. J. Comput. Biol. **17**(9), 1113–1128 (2010)

19. Zheng, C., Chen, E., Albert, V.A., Lyons, E., Sankoff, D.: Ancient eudicot hexaploidy meets ancestral eurosid gene order. BMC Genomics **14**(S7), S3 (2013)

A Fast Word Embedding Based Classifier to Profile Target Gene Databases in Metagenomic Samples

G. A. Arango-Argoty[1], L. S. Heath[1], A. Pruden[2], P. J. Vikesland[2], and L. Zhang[1](✉)

[1] Department of Computer Science, Virginia Tech, Blacksburg, VA, USA
lqzhang@vt.edu
[2] Department of Civil and Environmental Engineering, Virginia Tech, Blacksburg, VA, USA

Abstract. The functional profile of metagenomic samples allows the understanding of the role of the microbes in the environment. Sequence alignment of short reads against curated databases has been widely used to profile metagenomic samples. However, this method is time consuming and requires high computing resources. Although several alignment free methods based on k-mer composition have been developed in recent years, they still require a large amount of memory. In this paper, MetaMLP (**Meta**genomics **M**achine **L**earning **P**rofiler), a machine learning method that represents sequences into numerical vectors (embeddings) and uses a simple one hidden layer neural network is proposed to profile functional categories. Unlike other methods, MetaMLP enables partial matching through a reduced alphabet for sequence embeddings. MetaMLP is able to identify a larger number of reads compared to Diamond (one of the fastest sequence alignment methods) while maintaining high performance with a 0.99 precision and a 0.99 recall. MetaMLP can process 100 million reads in around 10 min in a laptop computer, a 50x speed up compared to Diamond. MetaMLP is freely available at https://bitbucket.org/gaarangoa/metamlp/src/master/.

Keywords: Word-embedding · Sequence alignment · Metagenomic · Gene profiling · Neural network

1 Introduction

The wide and rapid adoption of metagenomic sequencing in studying microbial diversity, antibiotic resistance, and other functional profiling poses serious computational challenges. The large amounts of data require development of computational tools that are both accurate and fast. Many sequence comparison algorithms such as BLAST [1], FASTA [2], HMMER [3], PSI-BLAST [4] have been introduced. BLAST is to date the most popular and trusted tool for sequence alignment. However, it is well known that BLAST does not scale well when comparing millions of sequences. The reason is that BLAST uses a computationally demanding strategy consisting of a seed and extend algorithm [5]. Although sequence alignment is considered the gold standard approach for sequence analysis, there are cases where this technique can produce dubious results [6].

© Springer Nature Switzerland AG 2021
S. K. Jha et al. (Eds.): ICCABS 2020, LNBI 12686, pp. 116–126, 2021.
https://doi.org/10.1007/978-3-030-79290-9_10

For instance, alignment-based methods assume that homologous sequences share a certain degree of conservation. Although this assumption is considered to be true when analyzing conserved domains, organisms such as viruses that exhibit high mutation rates challenge this collinearity principle. When analyzing short sequences (e.g., Illumina sequencing reads), the percentage of identity does not guarantee correctness. Highly identical sequences do not imply homology [7]. In the opposite case, sequences with less than 30% identity can potentially be considered as homologous [8].

DIAMOND [9], BLAT [10], USEARCH [11], and RAPSearch [12] are alternatives to BLASTX that can run much faster but with a loss of sensitivity. Particularly, the dramatic speed up of DIAMOND (20,000X over BLAST) is achieved by using a double indexing strategy, spaced seeds (longer seeds where not all positions are used) and a reduced alphabet. In detail, DIAMOND implements a seed and extend algorithm that first indexes both query and reference sequences. Then, the list of seeds in both the query and reference are linearly traversed to determine all the matched seeds with their locations. Finally, seeds are extended using the Smith-Waterman algorithm [13].

Alignment-free methods have been proposed as an alternative to quantify sequence similarity without performing sequence alignment [6, 14]. These methods do not use the seed and extend paradigm. Therefore, their computational complexity is often linear and only depends on the query sequence length. In next-generation sequencing, several alignment-free strategies have been developed for different applications, including transcript quantification (kallisto [15], sailfish [16], Salmon [17], RNA-Skim [18]), variant calling (ChimeRScope [19], FastGT [20]), de-novo genome assembly (minimap [21], MHAP [22]), and the profiling of metagenomics taxonomy using a k-mer matching approach (Kraken [23], Mash [24], CLARK [25], and stringMLST [26]).

The word embeddings technique is one of the most successful methods applied in natural language processing (NLP) where words can be represented as a numerical vectors. For instance, the Word2vec technique [27] uses a shallow two-layer neural network to train and aggregate word embeddings by using the continuous bag of words (CBOW) approach. Thus, identifying semantic associations between a target word and its context. The concept of using word vectors for representing protein/DNA sequences is not new and has been explored before. For instance, DNA2Vec [28] explores the associations between varying length k-mers to generate an embedding space that proved to correlate with sequence alignment. Yang et al. [29] explores the performance of word embeddings for classification of protein functions. Yan et al. demonstrated that k-mer embeddings outperformed other techniques. However, in both studies, embeddings are learnt in an unsupervised way. This means that the embeddings are computed first and then the classifier is built by using those embeddings. In this paper, MetaMLP, an alignment-free method that uses word embeddings to represent target protein databases is proposed for the functional profiling of metagenomic samples. The strategy behind MetaMLP relies on the CBOW model. However, the target word is replaced by the label or functional class of the sequence and the context words correspond to the k-mers and fragmented k-mers. Therefore, MetaMLP is a novel strategy that uses a combination of hash indexing, six open reading frame translation, a reduced amino acid alphabet and an embedding representation to process metagenomic data. In addition, MetaMLP was built up on top of the C++ FastText [30] library and consists of two main stages:

MetaMLP-index to process protein sequences to build a machine learning model and *MetaMLP-classify* to annotate reads from metagenomic sequencing data.

2 Methods

The overall structure of MetaMLP is shown in Fig. 1 and consists of two main components: **A**) An indexing stage that converts protein reference sequences into a word vector representation to train a classifier, and **B**) A prediction stage that processes short sequencing reads and classifies them into one of the predefined classes from the reference database.

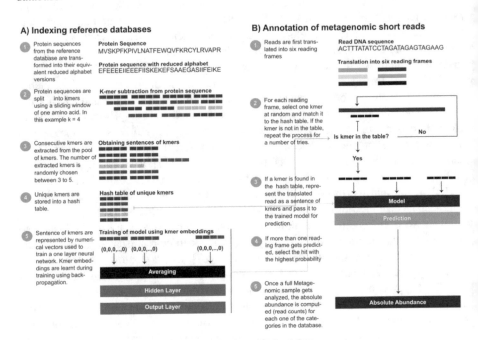

Fig. 1. Overview of MetaMLP.

2.1 Indexing Protein Reference Databases

Reference Database Preprocessing. To increase the chances of detecting sequences with mismatches, reference proteins are first transformed into their equivalent 10 amino acid alphabet version using the murphy. 10 alphabet representation used in Rapsearch (a [KR] [EDNQ] C G H [ILVM] [FYW] P [ST]) [31]. Then, k-mers of a fixed length are extracted from each protein sequence. However, to consider all k-mers within a sequence, a sliding window of one amino acid is used. Thus, each protein comprises k versions, each one corresponding to a different starting location [1, …, k]. Thereafter, a 'sentence' of k-mers is extracted by taking 3 to 5 consecutive k-mers (equivalent to reads of 100 to 150 bps, Fig. 1A). At the same time, a table with unique k-mers is built and stored for later to be used for filtering sequences that diverge greatly from the reference database during the prediction stage.

Training. MetaMLP uses the FastText implementation of the continuous bag of words (CBoW) technique to learn the semantic relations between protein sequences and their labels. Thus, proteins are represented as a series of k-mer sentences (analog to sentence of words in text documents). Then, it decomposes each k-mer within the sentences into a numerical representation (k-mer vector) (see Fig. 1A). Later, it computes the average of the k-mer vectors and passes it to a single hidden layer neural network. Finally, it outputs the probability distribution over the established classes by using a softmax layer. In addition, MetaMLP enables the bag of n-grams feature from FastText to capture partial information from the k-mers. These n-grams are sub sequences from the k-mers passed along with the full size k-mer allowing to identify k-mers with partial matching.

2.2 Prediction of Short Reads

MetaMLP is designed to efficiently profile metagenomic samples with millions of reads from short sequencing libraries against a target reference database. As reads are made of nucleotides, MetaMLP first translates each sequence into six reading frames. Then for each reading frame, a random k-mer is selected from its sequence and checked against the hash table that was built during the indexing stage. If a k-mer is found in the hash table, all k-mers are extracted from the read and classified using the trained CBoW model. If not, a new k-mer is randomly selected from the read at a different position. This process is repeated to a maximum number of tries defined by the user. If more than one reading frame gets classified, MetaMLP picks up the reading frame with the highest classification probability (see Fig. 1B).

Once a full metagenomic dataset is processed, MetaMLP counts the number of reads per class using a minimum probability cutoff defined by the user and reports an absolute abundance table. Additionally, MetaMLP also reports a fasta file containing the read name along with its classifications, probabilities and sequence. This file is useful for cases where MetaMLP is used as a filter to target a particular functional class.

2.3 Databases

Pathway Reference Database. Bacterial protein sequences from the Universal Protein Resource (UniProt) were downloaded and filtered, keeping only those proteins that have been manually curated, reviewed and contained evidence at the protein level. In total 20,161 proteins were obtained and 4,105 of those were annotated to at least one pathway. Lastly, pathways with less than 50 proteins were discarded to get a total of 3,216 proteins and 21 different pathways.

Antibiotic Resistance Database. MetaMLP was trained to identify short reads associated to Antibiotic Resistance Genes (ARGs) from metagenomic short sequencing data. Thus the DeepARG-DB-v2 database [32] containing a total of 12,260 sequences belonging to 30 antibiotic categories was downloaded. However, only antibiotic resistance categories with at least 50 protein sequences were considered for downstream analysis. Thus, a total of 12,147 proteins and 14 categories were used to train the MetaMLP model.

Gene Ontology Reference Database. Protein sequences associated to the biological process response to stress (GO:0006950) were downloaded from UniProt website. However, only bacterial curated sequences and biological processes with at least 100 sequences were considered for downstream analysis. In addition, the GO database comprises proteins with multiple associated labels. For instance, the protein sequence Q55002 is associated to response to antibiotic (GO:0046677) and translation (GO:0006412). Therefore, reads from this protein would be classified to both categories. However, as MetaMLP uses a softmax layer for prediction, it will distribute the probability between both categories. In an ideal scenario, both classes would have a probability of 0.5. This database was used to test the ability of MetaMLP to represent sequences associated to multiple labels.

2.4 True Positive Dataset

The pathway database was used to build a true positive database. Because MetaMLP uses amino acid sequences for training and nucleotide sequences for querying, it was necessary to identify the corresponding nucleotide sequences for each one of the proteins in the pathways database. Therefore, UniProt identifiers were cross referenced against the RefSeq database and a list of gene candidates were found. Then, those candidates were aligned to the protein sequences using Diamond BlastX with a 90% identity and a 90% overlap. If multiple alignments were obtained, the best hit was selected as the representative gene sequence for the target protein sequence. Thus, each entry in the database contained a respective gene sequence. Finally, the pathway database was randomly split into training (80%) and validation (20%). The training set was used to tune the model whereas the validation set was used only to test the trained model. Note that the training set corresponds to amino acid sequences whereas the validation set consists of nucleotide sequences. To simulate a library of short reads, sequences of 100bp long were randomly extracted from each nucleotide sequence from the validation dataset. Thus, a total of 35,751 short reads were generated.

Diamond is currently one of the most widely used tools for metagenomic analysis. Therefore, to evaluate the performance of MetaMLP, Diamond BlastX with the best hit approach was used. Diamond was run using a sequence alignment identity of 80%, whereas MetaMLP was set with a minimum probability of 0.8. Precision, Recall and F1 score were computed to measure the performance of both approaches.

2.5 False Positives Dataset

To test the ability of MetaMLP to filter out sequences that are not associated to any of the selected pathways (false positives), a synthetic dataset was constructed using the same number of reads from the true positive dataset. However, each nucleotide position on this dataset was randomly selected. This negative dataset was then run against MetaMLP and the best hit approach using Diamond with default parameters. Precision, recall and F1 score were computed to measure the performance of both methods.

2.6 Time and Memory Profiling

To evaluate the time performance and memory footprint of MetaMLP, a dataset of 100k, 1M, 10M and 100M reads were built by randomly extracting reads from a real metagenomic soil sample of 407,645,066 reads. This sample is under the SRA accession number SRR2901746 and corresponds to a 250bp long read sample from the Illumina HiSeq 2000 sequencer. Along with MetaMLP, Diamond was also run with the same datasets. Both methods were run with only one CPU enabled in the same Linux 16.4 environment.

2.7 Functional Annotation of Metagenomic Datasets

MetaMLP was used to profile four different environments comprising a total of 68 metagenomic samples through the functional composition analysis including: Pathways detection, response to stress, and antibiotic resistance composition. The 68 public available metagenomes were downloaded from the Sequence Read Archive (SRA) from the National Center for Biotechnology Information (NCBI) spanning four different environments as follows: 10 soil (**S**), 15 human gut (**HG**), 15 freshwater (**FW**) and 28 wastewater (**WW**) samples. Results from MetaMLP were compared against the best hit approach using Diamond BlastX with an identity cutoff of 80%.

For the GO reference database, MetaMLP was run with a permissive 0.5 minimum probability to retrieve multiple classifications. Relative abundance results were compared against those obtained using sequence alignment with Diamond BlastX at an 80% identity cutoff.

3 Results and Discussion

The sequence embedding strategy allows MetaMLP to represent amino acid sequences into numerical vectors (embedding dimension) by taking into account the distribution of the k-mers in the protein sequence as well as their labels. Thus, MetaMLP uses the supervised embedding implementation from FastText to learn these numerical vectors and minimize the distances between members of the same class and maximize the outer distance to other classes. For instance, proteins that belong to Beta-lactamase class are expected to cluster together and keep distant from members of other classes. Figure 2 shows the distribution of the MetaMLP embeddings in a two dimensional space generated by the t-SNE algorithm [33]. For targeted databases such as the ARG categories or pathways database, MetaMLP clustered categories according to their labels with a representative cohesion and separation (silhouette score: 0.56 and 0.62 for pathways and for ARGs respectively, Fig. 2A–B). Interestingly, in a complex classification problem represented by the GO database where proteins contain multiple labels, MetaMLP show a consistent distribution over the clusters and its corresponding categories. Clusters shown in Fig. 2C describes the relationship among different biological processes involved in response to stress. For example, proteins responding to antibiotics are also associated to other biological process such as response to toxic substances, pathogenesis, defense to virus, chemotaxis, response to DNA damage, among others. Such associations can be clearly seen from the embeddings visualization. Therefore, the embedding strategy adopted in MetaMLP is also suitable for representing reference databases where proteins contains multiple labels.

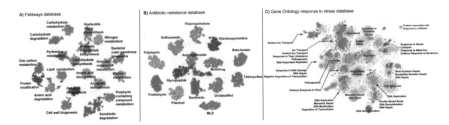

Fig. 2. The MetaMLP embeddings for different gene databases

3.1 Detection of True Positive Hits

The pathways database was used to assess the ability of MetaMLP to 1) discriminate between pathway-like reads and 2) to evaluate the performance of MetaMLP on classifying short sequences from a particular pathway. To compare the performance of MetaMLP, the best hit approach using Diamond BlastX was used. In total, MetaMLP was able to identify 10,433 (29%) pathway-like reads out of the total 35,751 with a probability greater than 0.8, whereas, the baseline approach was able to identify 8,695 (24%) reads out of the 35,751. Thus, MetaMLP was able to identify 5% more reads than the best hit approach at 80% identity cutoff. Further, both methods were compared for their positive predictions to evaluate their performance in discriminating reads from a particular pathway. As expected, the sequence alignment approach performed with a high average precision (0.99) and recall (1.00) whereas MetaMLP was also near to a perfect prediction with a 0.99 average precision and 0.99 average recall indicating the potential of the k-mer vectors to represent protein sequences to profile metagenomes. It is also worth mentioning that both MetaMLP and the best hit approach did not perform well for three categories (Aromatic compound metabolism, Bacterial outer membrane biogenesis, and xenobiotic degradation). Interestingly, the best hit approach was not able to identify any read for the bacterial outer membrane biogenesis when MetaMLP obtained a 1.00 precision but a low 0.13 recall indicating a high sensitivity of MetaMLP in discriminating true positives for this category but failing for false negatives. In terms of relative abundance, the read counts were highly correlated between the best hit approach and MetaMLP (Pearson correlation coefficient = 0.988), indicating that MetaMLP can correctly characterize the composition of the pathways in the simulated dataset.

3.2 Detection of False Positives Hits

A false positive refers to a read that does not belong to any pathway class but is predicted to a particular pathway. In this false positive scenario, MetaMLP was tested against the number of predicted random reads by counting how many out of the 35,751 negative reads were classified in any pathways. MetaMLP classified only two reads (0.005%) out of the 35,751 negative reads, indicating a very low false positive rate. As expected, the best hit approach did not produce any relevant alignment.

3.3 Time and Memory Usage of MetaMLP

The main advantage for using a classifier instead of performing a sequence alignment is the running time improvement. Results show that MetaMLP keeps an almost identical level of sensitivity compared to Diamond BlastX. However, the strength of MetaMLP relies on its speed. Table 1 shows the speed benchmarking over datasets with different number of reads. Note that MetaMLP is >50x times faster than Diamond for all the sample sizes. MetaMLP produces very similar results in terms of relative abundance using the ARGs database and pathway database with a correlation of 0.951 and 0.953, respectively. Note that in this test, MetaMLP identified 35% more ARG-like reads (253,370) compared to the number of reads (186,736) detected from Diamond BlastX. In addition, MetaMLP is also memory efficient, depending mostly on the size of the reference database. For instance, it requires a minimum RAM memory of 1.0 Gb to run the pathway database, 1.2 Gb the ARGs database and 2.8 Gb the GO database. When processing 100M reads, it required 1.7 Gb in total with the pathways database whereas Diamond BlastX required 6.68 Gb. The low memory usage in MetaMLP is a consequence of its classification strategy where reads are loaded in chunks of 10,000 reads for efficient I/O rate. Therefore, MetaMLP can be run on any personal computer without the need of a big computer cluster with a high amount of RAM memory.

Table 1. Time profiling of MetaMLP compared to Diamond BlastX for different sample sizes (s means seconds, m means minutes)

Number of reads	MetaMLP	Diamond
100,000	9 s	38 s
1,000,000	27 s	6 m
10,000,000	1 m	67 m
100,000,000	14 m	714 m

3.4 Functional Annotation of Different Environments

MetaMLP was run over the 67 real metagenomic samples processing a total of 2,186,933,071 reads. MetaMLP was able to predict 2,343,026 as ARG-like reads in 710 min using only one CPU, whereas Diamond BlastX identified 2,003,050 reads taking a total of 5,256 min using 20 CPUs. The average correlation of the abundances between Diamond and MetaMLP was of 0.94 (0.88 log transformed abundance). Interestingly, human gut microbiota and wastewater were the two environments where both methods had the highest correlation with respect to their log transformed abundance (0.96, 0.93 respectively) whereas soil and freshwater had each a correlation of 0.83.

3.5   Observation of MetaMLP Annotations Against an Extensive Metagenomics Study

An extensive study carried out by Pal et al. [34] uses over >800 metagenomic samples spanning several environments with a sequence alignment strategy at a 90% identity cut-off for annotation. This study (named Pal800 for simplicity) has shown that the human gut microbiota is one of the environments with the highest relative abundance compared to other microbiomes (soil, wastewater and freshwater). Concordantly, when MetaMLP was run over the 68 real metagenomic samples using the GO database, it also profiled the human gut microbiome as the highest relative abundance for the response to antibiotic process. Note that Pal800 used a curated ARG database and did not consider the inclusion of false positives. Moreover, their GO analysis only provides a general overview of the functional composition of those environments. In contrast, a more detailed analysis was obtained by looking at the results from MetaMLP using the specialized ARGs database. Overall, the same trend was observed when comparing both analysis (MetaMLP, Pal800). For example, the tetracycline category had the highest relative abundance in the human microbiome, sulfonamide shows the highest relative abundance in the wastewater environment, the relative abundance of the beta-lactamase class was higher in the freshwater compared to the wastewater and both are higher than human gut and soil environments. Pal800 also performed a composition profile of the mobile genetic elements present in the microbiomes. It has shown that wastewater, freshwater and soil environments had a higher relative abundance compared to the human gut. Interestingly, for MetaMLP the GO response to stress database conveyed a similar trend in relative abundance for the biological process "establishment of competence for transformation". This term is associated with genetic transfer between organisms and is described by the GO consortium as the process where exogenous DNA is acquired by a bacterium. In summary, despite only using 67 real metagenomes, the functional annotation based on MetaMLP described a very similar trending for relative abundances when compared to the Pal800 study, indicating a real scenario usage of MetaMLP.

4   Conclusions

MetaMLP is an alignment-free method for profiling metagenomic samples to specific target group of proteins (e.g., ARGs, pathways, GO terms) using a machine learning classifier. It uses sequence embeddings to represent protein/DNA sequences as numerical vectors and a linear classifier to discriminate between protein functions. Results show that MetaMLP has a comparable performance to the alignment-based method Diamond, and tends to identify more reads. Remarkably, MetaMLP is around 50x faster than Diamond. MetaMLP can be trained using any collection of protein sequences (reference database) and has a very low memory footprint for the specialized databases used in this paper. Finally, MetaMLP is open sourced and freely available at https://bitbucket.org/gaarangoa/metamlp/src/master/.

Acknowledgements. We thank the support from the USDA National Institute of Food and Agriculture competitive Grant 2017-68003-26498, the U.S. National Science Foundation Partnership in International Research and Education Award # 1545756, and the U.S. National Science Foundation Award # 2004751.

References

1. Altschul, S.F., et al.: Basic local alignment search tool. J. Mol. Biol. **215**(3), 403–410 (1990)
2. Pearson, W.R.: [5] Rapid and sensitive sequence comparison with FASTP and FASTA (1990)
3. Finn, R.D., Clements, J., Eddy, S.R.: HMMER web server: interactive sequence similarity searching. Nucleic Acids Res. **39**(suppl_2), W29–W37 (2011)
4. Altschul, S.F., et al.: Gapped BLAST and PSI-BLAST: a new generation of protein database search programs. Nucleic Acids Res. **25**(17), 3389–3402 (1997)
5. Li, H., Homer, N.: A survey of sequence alignment algorithms for next-generation sequencing. Brief. Bioinform. **11**(5), 473–483 (2010)
6. Zielezinski, A., et al.: Alignment-free sequence comparison: benefits, applications, and tools. Genome Biol. **18**(1), 186 (2017)
7. Bengtsson-Palme, J., Larsson, D.J., Kristiansson, E.: Using metagenomics to investigate human and environmental resistomes. J. Antimicrob. Chemother. **72**(10), 2690–2703 (2017)
8. Pearson, W.R.: An introduction to sequence similarity ("homology") searching. Curr Protoc Bioinformatics, Chapter 3: p. Unit 3 1 (2013)
9. Buchfink, B., Xie, C., Huson, D.H.: Fast and sensitive protein alignment using DIAMOND. Nat. Methods **12**(1), 59 (2015)
10. Kent, W.J.: BLAT—the BLAST-like alignment tool. Genome Res. **12**(4), 656–664 (2002)
11. Edgar, R.: USEARCH: ultra-fast sequence analysis (2015)
12. Ye, Y., Choi, J.-H., Tang, H.: RAPSearch: a fast protein similarity search tool for short reads. BMC Bioinform. **12**(1), 159 (2011)
13. Pearson, W.R.: Searching protein sequence libraries: comparison of the sensitivity and selectivity of the Smith-Waterman and FASTA algorithms. Genomics **11**(3), 635–650 (1991)
14. Vinga, S., Almeida, J.: Alignment-free sequence comparison—a review. Bioinformatics **19**(4), 513–523 (2003)
15. Weijers, S., et al.: KALLISTO: cost effective and integrated optimization of the urban wastewater system Eindhoven. Water Pract. Technol. **7**(2), wpt2012036 (2012)
16. Patro, R., Mount, S.M., Kingsford, C.: Sailfish enables alignment-free isoform quantification from RNA-seq reads using lightweight algorithms. Nat. Biotechnol. **32**(5), 462 (2014)
17. Patro, R., Duggal, G., Kingsford, C.: Accurate, fast, and model-aware transcript expression quantification with Salmon. bioRxiv, 21592 (2015)
18. Zhang, Z., Wang, W.: RNA-Skim: a rapid method for RNA-Seq quantification at transcript level. Bioinformatics **30**(12), i283–i292 (2014)
19. Li, Y., et al.: ChimeRScope: a novel alignment-free algorithm for fusion transcript prediction using paired-end RNA-Seq data. Nucleic Acids Res. gkx315 (2017)
20. Pajuste, F.-D., et al.: FastGT: an alignment-free method for calling common SNVs directly from raw sequencing reads. Sci. Rep. **7**(1), 2537 (2017)
21. Li, H.: Minimap and miniasm: fast mapping and de novo assembly for noisy long sequences. Bioinformatics **32**(14), 2103–2110 (2016)
22. Berlin, K., et al.: Assembling large genomes with single-molecule sequencing and locality-sensitive hashing. Nat. Biotechnol. **33**(6), 623 (2015)
23. Wood, D.E., Salzberg, S.L.: Kraken: ultrafast metagenomic sequence classification using exact alignments. Genome Biol. **15**(3), R46 (2014)
24. Ondov, B.D., et al.: Mash: fast genome and metagenome distance estimation using MinHash. Genome Biol. **17**(1), 132 (2016)
25. Ounit, R., et al.: CLARK: fast and accurate classification of metagenomic and genomic sequences using discriminative k-mers. BMC Genomics **16**(1), 236 (2015)
26. Gupta, A., Jordan, I.K., Rishishwar, L.: stringMLST: a fast k-mer based tool for multilocus sequence typing. Bioinformatics **33**(1), 119–121 (2016)

27. Goldberg, Y., Levy, O.: word2vec Explained: deriving Mikolov et al.'s negative-sampling word-embedding method. arXiv preprint arXiv:1402.3722 (2014)
28. Ng, P.: dna2vec: Consistent vector representations of variable-length k-mers. arXiv preprint arXiv:1701.06279 (2017)
29. Yang, K.K., et al.: Learned protein embeddings for machine learning. Bioinformatics **34**(15), 2642–2648 (2018)
30. Joulin, A., et al.: Bag of tricks for efficient text classification. arXiv preprint arXiv:1607.01759 (2016)
31. Zhao, Y., Tang, H., Ye, Y.: RAPSearch2: a fast and memory-efficient protein similarity search tool for next-generation sequencing data. Bioinformatics **28**(1), 125–126 (2011)
32. Arango-Argoty, G., et al.: DeepARG: a deep learning approach for predicting antibiotic resistance genes from metagenomic data. Microbiome **6**(1), 23 (2018)
33. Maaten, L.v.d., Hinton, G.: Visualizing data using t-SNE. J. Mach. Learn. Res. **9**, 2579–2605 (2008)
34. Pal, C., et al.: The structure and diversity of human, animal and environmental resistomes. Microbiome **4**(1), 54 (2016)

Clustering Based Identification of SARS-CoV-2 Subtypes

Andrew Melnyk⬤, Fatemeh Mohebbi⬤, Sergey Knyazev⬤, Bikram Sahoo⬤,
Roya Hosseini⬤, Pavel Skums⬤, Alex Zelikovsky$^{(\boxtimes)}$⬤, and Murray Patterson$^{(\boxtimes)}$⬤

Department of Computer Science, Georgia State University, Atlanta, GA, USA
alexz@cs.gsu.edu, mpatterson30@gsu.edu

Abstract. With the availability of more than half a million SARS-CoV-2 sequences and counting, many approaches have recently appeared which aim to leverage this information towards understanding the genomic diversity and dynamics of this virus. Early approaches involved building transmission networks or phylogenetic trees, the latter for which scalability becomes more of an issue with each day, due to its high computational complexity.

In this work, we propose an alternative approach based on clustering sequences to identify novel subtypes of SARS-CoV-2 using methods designed for haplotyping intra-host viral populations. We assess this approach using cluster entropy, a notion which very naturally captures the underlying process of viral mutation—the first time entropy was used in this context. Using our approach, we were able to identify the well-known B.1.1.7 subtype from the sequences of the EMBL-EBI (UK) database, and also show that the associated cluster is consistent with a measure of fitness. This demonstrates that our approach as a viable and scalable alternative to unveiling trends in the spread of SARS-CoV-2.

Keywords: Clustering · Viral strains · Viral subtypes · Entropy · Fitness

1 Background

A novel coronavirus, responsible for severe acute respiratory syndrome (SARS-CoV-2) was first detected in Wuhan, China at the end of 2019 [35, 36], and its outbreak was declared a pandemic in March 2020 by the World Health Organization (WHO). As of the end of 2020, this virus was found in at least 219 countries, with over 70 million infected [34], and this situation continues to change on a weekly basis. As the virus spreads across the globe, it continues to mutate, as evidenced by the more than half a million sequences that have been collected by public databases such as GISAID [12] and COG-UK [10]. This mutational variability can be used to understand the genomic diversity and dynamics of SARS-CoV-2, and to generate hypotheses on how the virus has spread. Various types of approaches exist in order to leverage this sequence data, such as building transmission networks of infection. An example of such an approach is [29], where the authors show that the network is *scale-free*—few genomic variants are responsible for the majority of possible transmissions. Other approaches involve the construction of a phylogenetic tree [14, 24] of evolution of the virus. In this latter

© Springer Nature Switzerland AG 2021
S. K. Jha et al. (Eds.): ICCABS 2020, LNBI 12686, pp. 127–141, 2021.
https://doi.org/10.1007/978-3-030-79290-9_11

case of tree building approaches, the number of sequences currently available is already two orders of magnitude beyond what can be processed, at least all at once [14,24, 33]. All of these approaches are, moreover, confounded by the presence of *gaps* in the sequences, which are prevalent even after some combination of alignment, error-correction, filtering of unreliable reads, trimming, *etc..*, is applied [12,19].

A third alternative to studying the mutational variability of SARS-CoV-2 could make use of the information obtained by *clustering* sets of sequences. While individual sequences are often unique, the sheer number of sequences available (*e.g.*, in GISAID) is expected to nonetheless unveil meaningful groups and trends. Moreover, since most clustering techniques are much faster than, *e.g.*, tree building [14,24], it can easily scale to the full size of the current datasets. There is a natural correspondence between clusters of similar sequences and *subtypes*, such as the so-called B.1.1.7, which was first detected very recently in the United Kingdom [32]. While the B.1.1.7 subtype (or variant) only differs from the SARS-CoV-2 lineage by a few dozen mutations, it has been shown to be between 40–80% more transmissible [32]—see [13] for the most recent updates. This motivates the early detection and characterization of future subtypes which have the potential to be more contagious, based on how current subtypes, *i.e.*, their sequence content, correlate with contagiousness.

In this work, we cluster sets of sequences from both GISAID [12] and EMBL-EBI [1]. We use, as cluster *centers*, the subtypes inferred by CliqueSNV [21]—a tool which is designed for finding viral variants from sequencing data. We show that this approach outperforms standard approaches for clustering (categorical data) such as k-modes, in terms of the cluster *entropy* [22] attained. While entropy is an ideal measure of the quality of a clustering in this context, this is the first time (that we know of) that entropy was used in the context of finding viral subtypes. We validate our clustering approach from an experimental point of view by correctly detecting (based on metadata) the B.1.1.7 subtype from EMBL-EBI (UK) [1] sequences taken from the beginning of October to the middle of December. To further strengthen this result, we assess the selective *fitness* of a subtype, based on the number of sequences of the corresponding cluster, and how this changes over time [28]. We show that the cluster obtained from our approach corresponding to the B.1.1.7 subtype consistently has the highest fitness over time. This illustrates the utility of our approach for finding novel subtypes which have the potential to become pervasive in the population. Additionally, we use the information from clustering to patch gaps in the sequences. This applies in particular to sequences collected before March, when SARS-CoV-2 sequencing efforts were in their infancy. Since cluster entropy is so fitting to this setting, we aim to fill gaps in sequences with the objective of minimizing the entropy of the result.

This paper is structured as follows. In Sect. 2, we detail our approach to clustering and gap filling. In Sect. 3, we specify several ways of assessing these approaches, namely, cluster entropy and the fitness coefficient. In Sect. 4, we give the results of our clustering and gap filling approach on the GISAID and EMBL-EBI datasets. Section 5 then concludes the paper with a discussion of the contributions of our approach, in light of these results.

2 Clustering Methods

We cluster sequences of SARS-CoV-2 based purely on sequence content, and under no *a priori* hypothesis about the relationships between these sequences, *i.e.*, it is unsupervised. In this study we use sequences from the GISAID [12] database, as well as that of EMBL-EBI [1]. The clustering techniques we use are described in the following.

2.1 CliqueSNV Based Clustering

For clustering viral subtypes, we propose to use existing tools that are used to identify subtypes of the intra-host viral populations from NGS data reviewed in [20], *e.g.*, Savage [4], PredictHaplo [25], aBayesQR [2], *etc.* In this work, the setting is slightly different, where the data consists of large collections of *inter-host* consensus sequences gathered from different regions and countries around the world [1, 12]. We expect, however, that such tools are appropriate at this scale, that is, the "host" is now an entire region or country, and we reconstruct the variants and their dynamics within these regions or countries. The SARS-CoV-2 sequences in GISAID are consensus sequences of approximate length 30K. Such sequences by quality and especially length have similar properties as PacBio reads. We choose CliqueSNV since it performed very well on PacBio long reads [21]. We use default parameters to run CliqueSNV, setting the minimum cluster frequency to be at least 1% of the population.

2.2 k-modes Clustering

We also considered known general techniques for clustering from the literature as a baseline for comparison. Since we are clustering sequences, which are on the *categories* A, C, G, T (and –, a gap), we chose k-modes [15, 16] for this purpose. This approach is almost identical to k-means [3, 23], but it is based on the notion of *mode* (rather than Euclidean mean), making it appropriate for clustering categorical data. Indeed, the Euclidean mean of three nucleotides has little meaning in this context, and may not even be well-defined. An example of the latter is when the "distance" from A to G is different than from G to A. A similar observation was made in the context cancer mutation profiles [9] in the form of absence/presence information. Treating these as categories in using k-modes (rather than as 0's and 1's in using k-means) resulted in a clustering approach [7] that, when used as a preprocessing step, allowed cancer phylogeny building methods to attain a higher accuracy [8], and in some cases with much lower runtimes [17].

The *mode* q of a cluster C of sequences is another "sequence" (on A, C, G, T, –) which minimizes

$$D(C, q) = \sum_{s \in C} d(s, q), \qquad (1)$$

where d is some dissimilarity measure (such as Hamming distance) between the sequences we are considering. Note that q is not necessarily an element of C. Aside from finding the mode instead of the Euclidean mean, the k-modes algorithm operates similarly to k-means, following the same iteration:

1. Initialize cluster centers (or centroids);
2. Assign each sequence to the closest center based on dissimilarity d;
3. For each cluster resulting from this assignment, find its (new) center (Eq. 1); and
4. Return to step 2 until convergence (clusters do not change between 2 and 3).

In this work, we use k-modes with the following six combinations of different settings. We first initialize cluster centers (1) by:

(a) choosing k random sequences from the dataset;
(b) choosing k centers that are maximally pairwise distant from each other; or
(c) using the centers (the subtypes) that were found by CliqueSNV.

Then, the dissimilarity d that we use is either the (i) Hamming distance, or (ii) TN-93 distance [30].

2.3　MeShClust

For comparison purposes, we also apply methods intended to cluster metagenomics and multiviral sequencing data. We clustered the sequences using MeShClust [18], an unsupervised machine learning method that aims to provide highly accurate clusterings while not depending on any user-specified similarity parameters. However, the given approach is intended to be used with datasets that contain multiple viral genomes. In particular, it was validated on a multiviral dataset, containing 96 viral genomes with an average length of 3K–12K bp. On the other hand, SARS-CoV-2 datasets usually contain several hundred thousand sequences of a single virus with genome lengths averaging around 30K bp.

2.4　Gap Filling

Finally, the set of SARS-CoV-2 sequences that we analyze contain missing nucleotides due to gaps or deletions. This is particularly true with the GISAID dataset which includes the range of collection dates from December 2019 to the end of March 2020, when sequencing, alignment, *etc.*, were less refined. This effort to fill the gaps is further confounded by the presence of deletions, which could be confused with gaps.

Here, we attempt to use the centers (or consensus sequences) of the clusters we find in order to perform gap filling. That is, rather than uniformly filling all sequences with, *e.g.*, a reference genome, for each individual sequence, we first find the cluster center that it is closest to, and then fill the gaps based on this center.

3　Assessment of Clustering Viral Subtypes

Here, we present two methods for assessing a clustering. The first is cluster entropy, an internal evaluation criterion that is very suited to this setting. The second is a measure of the selective fitness of clusters, based on how they change over time.

3.1 Cluster Entropy

Since we are comparing various clusterings of our data without a ground truth, we need to consider an *internal* evaluation criteria. Most of the commonly used criteria require some notion of a *distance* (or dissimilarity measure) between the objects being clustered. For example, criteria such as the Calinski-Harabasz Index [6] or the Gap Statistic [31] rely on the Euclidean distance, while the Davies-Bouldin Index [11] or the Silhouette Coefficient [26] require this distance to be a *metric*. In our setting, with the categories A, C, G, T and also the *gap* (–), it is unsure even what the distance between two categories (*e.g.*, A to G) would be, let alone whether this distance is Euclidean, or a metric.

The cluster *entropy* [22], a criterion that was shown to generalize any distance-based criterion, does not require a distance at all. This is ideal in our case, since it does not make any assumptions about the relationships between the categories A, C, G, T and gap (–). Since the information about such relationships is so lacking in this context, forcing an arbitrary set of assumptions in using a distance-based criterion may only bias the resulting analysis. Moreover, cluster entropy very naturally captures our setting: that the population of viral sequences comes from a number of subtypes. This is because cluster entropy can be formally derived using a likelihood principle based on Bernoulli mixture models. In these mixture models, the observed data are thought of as coming from a number of different latent classes. In [22], the authors prove that minimizing cluster entropy is equivalent to maximizing the likelihood that set of objects are generated from a set of (k) classes. This is very akin to this setting: the set of objects are viral sequences, and they come from a set of k subtypes.

Cluster entropy relates closely to the widely-used notion of *sequence logo* [27]: a graphical representation of a set of aligned sequences which conveys, at each position, both the relative frequency of each base (or residue), and the amount of information (the entropy) in bits. Hence, a clustering of viral sequences of low entropy gives rise to a confident set of sequence logos (in terms of information), and can therefore shed light on the possible biological function of viral subtype that each such logo (or related motif) represents.

Formally, we have a set S of *aligned* sequences over a set X of columns. A given column is then also a (vertical) "sequence" on the categories A, C, G, T and gap (–). Let $\mathcal{N} = \{A, C, G, T\}$, the four nucleotides, not counting the gap (–) character. Using the notation of [22], the entropy $\hat{H}_x(C)$ of a set C of rows (a cluster of sequences) for a column $x \in X$ then

$$\hat{H}_x(C) = -\sum_{s \in C} \sum_{a \in \mathcal{N}} p_x(s = a) \log p_x(s = a). \tag{2}$$

Note that $p_x(s = a)$—the probability that a sequence $s \in C$ has nucleotide a in column x—essentially amounts to the relative *frequency* of nucleotide $a \in \mathcal{N}$ in C in this column x. The entropy $\hat{H}_X(C)$ of set C of rows in a set X of columns is then

$$\hat{H}_X(C) = \sum_{x \in X} \hat{H}(x), \tag{3}$$

that is, we simply sum up the entropies of the columns. Since the set of X columns will always the set of SNV sites of our sequences in this context, we will use simply $\hat{H}(C)$ from hereon in. This way, $\hat{H}(C)$ is understood to be the entropy of a set (a cluster) of sequences. The *expected* entropy [22] of a clustering $\mathbb{C} = C_1, \ldots, C_k$ of sequences is then

$$H(\mathbb{C}) = \frac{1}{n} \sum_{i=1}^{k} n_i \hat{H}(C_i), \tag{4}$$

where $n_i = |C_i|$, the number of elements in cluster C_i, and n is the total number of sequences. For completeness, the total entropy of a clustering is simply the sum

$$T(\mathbb{C}) = \sum_{i=1}^{k} \hat{H}(C_i) \tag{5}$$

of the individual entropies of each cluster (not weighted by n_i).

3.2   Fitness

We use a mathematical model proposed in [28] for the calculation of a numerical measure of the *fitness* of a quasispecies. This model is used here to calculate the fitness of a cluster, based on how its size (number of sequences it contains) changes over a series of time steps. For a given set of clusters $C_1, \ldots, C_k$, $X_i(t)$ denotes the size of cluster C_i at a particular time step t. The fitness coefficient is calculated using h_i which is the cumulative sum of the X_i. Therefore, $h(t) = \sum_{i=1}^{k} h_i(t)$ is the total infected population size at time t. This $h_i(t)$ is then normalized over $h(t)$ and denoted by $u_i(t)$, that is,

$$u_i(t) = \frac{h_i(t)}{\sum_{i=1}^{k} h_i(t)}. \tag{6}$$

Using cubic splines, $u_i(t)$ and $h(t)$ are interpolated over the time period and the derivatives $\dot{u}_i(t)$ and $\dot{h}(t)$ are calculated. The *fitness function* g_i, for each cluster C_i is then defined as

$$g_i(t) = \frac{\dot{u}_i(t)}{u_i(t)} + \frac{\dot{h}(t)}{h(t)}. \tag{7}$$

The *fitness coefficient* r_i, which is the average fitness over the time period T (composed of the time steps t) for cluster C_i is then

$$r_i = \frac{1}{T} \int_1^T g_i(t) dt. \tag{8}$$

In order to reduce sampling error, we use the Poisson distribution to draw random samples. For each cluster at each time step, a sufficiently large number of random samples is drawn from the Poisson distribution on $X_i(t)$ as the expectation of the interval. Then $X_i(t)$ is replaced by the mean value of these random samples. This is repeated a sufficiently large number of times (*e.g.*, 100) to calculate a set of Poisson-distributed sizes. The fitness coefficient calculation is then applied on each separately and a confidence interval (*e.g.*, 95%) of this fitness coefficient is obtained.

4   Results

Here we report the results of our approach of clustering and gap filling using 2 datasets. The first dataset consists of sequences submitted to the GISAID [12] database from December 2019 to November 2020. This dataset contains sequences from all over the world. The second dataset consists of sequences submitted to the EMBL-EBI [1, 10] database from the beginning of October 2020 to the middle of December 2020. This dataset comprises sequences from various locations in the UK during the period of rapid spread of the B.1.1.7 subtype. For both datasets, we align the sequences and trim the first and last 50 bp of the aligned sequences.

4.1   Analysis of GISAID Data

Using our technique involving CliqueSNV, we clustered the data to identify at most 66 subtypes, which vary in proportion between December 2019 and November 2020. In this case, a k of 66 was needed in order for the minimum cluster frequency to be at least 1% of the population. We report the relative distributions of these different subtypes in Fig. 1 and Fig. 2, in a similar way to that of Fig. 3 of [24].

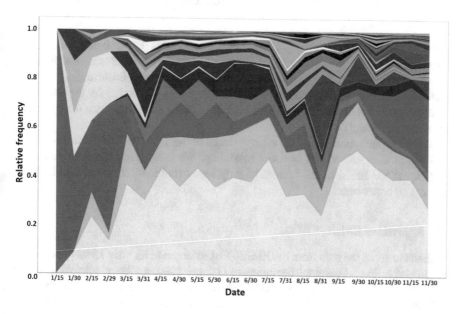

Fig. 1. Subtype distribution (GISAID dataset, 15-day window, relative count)

Table 1 gives an assessment of the various clusterings computed, in terms of both the expected entropy (Eq. 4) and total entropy (Eq. 5). While any form of clustering achieves a better expected (and total) entropy than not clustering at all, our CliqueSNV based approach tends to outperform all other forms of clustering using either Hamming

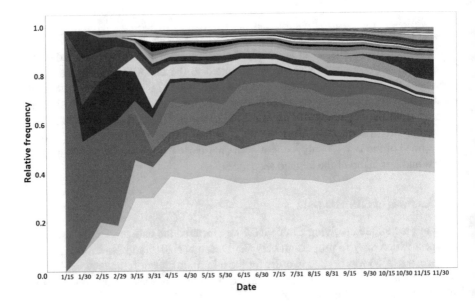

Fig. 2. Subtype distribution (GISAID dataset, cumulative, relative count).

or TN-93 distance. MeShClust [18] was not run due to this dataset being prohibitively large (see Sect. 2.3). Finally, by filling gaps in sequences based on the closest cluster center, we achieve an even lower expected (and total) entropy. This illustrates the appropriateness of this cluster based approach for filling gaps. For example, the entropy of the dataset without clustering remained high after filling gaps (based on the consensus for the entire dataset).

Table 2 reports runtimes of the various stages of this analysis, and Table 3 compares runtimes of CliqueSNV and k-modes clustering. We note, given the latter table, that our CliqueSNV based method had a slightly lower runtime than k-modes, despite it performing better overall.

4.2   Analysis of EMBL-EBI Data

We then clustered the data from the EMBL-EBI database to identify 15 subtypes which vary in proportion between the beginning of October 2020 and the middle of December 2020. Since the data here are over a shorter time span (*i.e.*, are smaller) and are more uniform, a k of 15 was sufficient for the minimum cluster frequency to be at least 1% of the population in this case. It is for the same reason that it was feasible to run MeShClust [18] in this case, even though it was only able to infer 3 clusters from this dataset.

Table 4 shows the F-1 score for all analyzed methods. CliqueSNV outperformed all other methods, as it produced a clustering with all of the B.1.1.7 sequences residing in a single cluster, while only 1.30% of the sequences in this cluster did not belong to the B.1.1.7 subtype. For k-modes, sequences belonging to the B.1.1.7 subtype were

Table 1. The expected entropy (Eq. 4) and total entropy (Eq. 5) of the GISAID sequences without clustering (*i.e.*, considered as a single cluster containing all sequences), and when clustering using each of the six combinations of settings mentioned in Sect. 2.2, both without filling gaps and with gap filling. The best performing method (lowest entropy) in each case is in bold font.

k-modes setting (initialization, distance)	Without gap filling		With gap filling	
	Expected entropy	Total entropy	Expected entropy	Total entropy
Without clustering	9536.89	9536.89	8417.89	8417.89
Random centers, Hamming	123.00	3170.60	109.21	2474.30
Random centers, TN-93	127.32	4401.18	111.05	3470.03
Pairwise distant, Hamming	422.65	4651.23	294.98	3629.47
Pairwise distant, TN-93	273.34	3500.14	256.44	3007.07
CliqueSNV, Hamming	**110.58**	2585.29	**90.42**	2308.95
CliqueSNV, TN-93	121.87	**2379.46**	100.85	**2117.40**

Table 2. Runtimes of the different stages of the algorithm for the GISAID dataset, which contains 199240 sequences. All stages were executed on a PC with an Intel(R) Xeon(R) CPU X5550 2.67GHz x2 with 8 cores per CPU, DIMM DDR3 1333 MHz RAM 4 Gb x12, and running the CentOS 6.4 operating system.

Algorithm stage	Time in seconds
CliqueSNV (inferring subtypes)	2405.08
CliqueSNV (finding closest subtypes)	2324.34
Gap filling	2740.32
Entropy computation	1254.22
Total	8723.96

Table 3. Runtimes of CliqueSNV and k-modes clustering using random centers and Hamming distance for the GISAID dataset, which contains 199240 sequences. Both methods were executed on the same PC mentioned in Table 2.

Clustering method	Time in seconds
CliqueSNV	4729.42
k-modes	4922.44

Table 4. F-1 score for CliqueSNV, k-modes and MeShClust. The **F-1 score major** is the F-1 score when only considering the cluster with the largest number of B.1.1.7 sequences, while **F-1 score all** is the F-1 score when considering all clusters containing B.1.1.7 sequences.

Method	F-1 score major	F-1 score all
Clique SNV	0.99	0.99
k-modes	0.24	0.003
MeShClust	0.11	0.11

spread over five clusters, with one cluster corresponding to 97.45% of these sequences. In this cluster, 86.54% of the sequences did not belong to the B.1.1.7 subtype, however. MeShClust produced a clustering with all of the B.1.1.7 sequences residing in one cluster, while 90.68% of the sequences in this cluster did not belong to the B.1.1.7 subtype.

We report the relative distributions of these different subtypes in Fig. 3. We report a weekly moving average, since a weekly oscillation in SARS-CoV-2 data has been noted in [5]. One will notice, in Fig. 3, the sharp increase of the relative proportion of a certain subtype (in red) to more than a third of the population. We confirm from metadata, that this indeed corresponds to the B.1.1.7 variant that was first identified in studies such as [32].

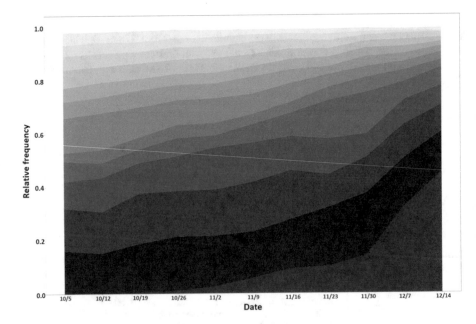

Fig. 3. Subtype distribution (EMBL-EBI dataset, weekly window, relative count), produced by CliqueSNV. The red subtype contributes to sequences that correspond to the B.1.1.7 lineage.

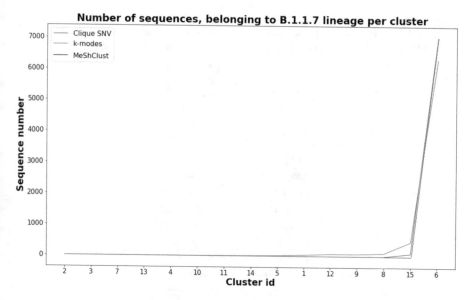

Fig. 4. The number of sequences belonging to the B.1.1.7 lineage per cluster for CliqueSNV, k-modes clustering and MeShClust. For CliqueSNV, all sequences are contained in 1 cluster (out of a total of 15). The k-modes clustering, on the other hand, reported that B.1.1.7 sequences are contained in 13 out of 15 clusters, with counts ranging from 1 to 6327 sequences per cluster. Finally, MeShClust was only able to produce 3 clusters, where one cluster contained all B.1.1.7 sequences (with 90.86% of the sequences in this cluster not belonging to this lineage).

Figure 4 gives the number of sequences from Fig. 3 that belong to this B.1.1.7 lineage by mid December 2020, which shows how accurately our approach has detected this subtype. For completeness, we report the results for gap filling in this case. The expected entropy for the gap-filled clustering is 75.73 for CliqueSNV, and 94.16 for k-modes, while total entropy is 986.48 for CliqueSNV and 2074.12 for k-modes. Entropy results for MeShClust are not reported since it only found 3 clusters. This analysis illustrates the ability of our clustering approach to identify subtypes which are known in the literature. Interestingly enough, the study of [32] is based on an approach of building a phylogenetic tree—this demonstrates our approach, which is based on clustering sequences, as a viable alternative.

Because our method detected one subtype which tends to dominate the population in this EMBL-EBI data, we wanted to see if this is consistent with a cluster-based fitness coefficient, *i.e.*, that of Sect. 3.2. In this case, we have $k = 15$ clusters, and we chose our time steps t to be intervals of one week over the period of the beginning of October to the middle of December. The size $X_i(t)$ of each cluster C_i in each week t was obtained, and each fitness coefficient r_i was computed accordingly (Eq. 8). In order to reduce sampling error, we drew 2000 random samples from the Poisson distribution on $X_i(t)$ according to Sect. 3.2. We repeated this 100 times, and we report the 95% confidence interval of the resulting coefficients of the clusters obtained with CliqueSNV centers using Hamming distance in Table 5, and using TN-93 distance in Table 6. We note that

Table 5. The 95% confidence interval of the fitness coefficient of each of the 15 clusters of the EMBL-EBI data obtained using CliqueSNV centers and Hamming distance. The cluster (number 6) with the highest fitness is in bold font, and corresponds to the B.1.1.7 subtype.

Cluster	Interval lower bound	Interval upper bound
1	0.016738872	0.016740732
2	0.048094793	0.04811301
3	0.03496386	0.035002021
4	0.047263532	0.047277361
5	0.014669158	0.014671058
6	**0.083354305**	**0.083409274**
7	0.02608419	0.026103458
8	0.041597557	0.041607292
9	0.066545115	0.066795373
10	0.045460704	0.045478018
11	0.015351276	0.015355419
12	0.029337299	0.029350051
13	0.049745178	0.049775704
14	0.008006433	0.008007678
15	0.013760131	0.013762324

Table 6. The 95% confidence interval of the fitness coefficient of each of the 15 clusters of the EMBL-EBI data obtained using CliqueSNV centers and TN-93 distance. The cluster (number 6) with the highest fitness is in bold font, and corresponds to the B.1.1.7 subtype.

Cluster	Interval lower bound	Interval upper bound
1	0.017183656	0.017185731
2	0.034293094	0.034331868
3	0.034447719	0.034479513
4	0.058367389	0.058395131
5	0.015729171	0.015731727
6	**0.081862323**	**0.08193304**
7	0.021651118	0.021659687
8	0.041761956	0.041788087
9	0.037012668	0.037036312
10	0.036169998	0.036178391
11	0.015727056	0.015730951
12	0.028816624	0.028835135
13	0.046192409	0.046213525
14	0.00913054	0.009132086
15	0.014634381	0.014637622

similar results are obtained with either distance. In any case, these coefficients confirm that the cluster with ID 6, identified in Fig. 4 to correspond to this B.1.1.7 subtype, is by far the most fit. This highlights the ability of our clustering based approach for detecting, based purely on sequence content, novel subtypes which have the potential of becoming dominant in the population.

5 Conclusions

In this work, we propose a novel method for identifying subtypes of SARS-CoV-2 by clustering the sequences of the virus. The first novelty of this approach is the use of a method (CliqueSNV) which was designed to discover viral subtypes from an intra-host population (*e.g.*, a single patient), to detect subtypes within an large inter-host population, *i.e.*, those sequences submitted to GISAID. The other novelty of our approach is the use of the cluster entropy criterion to assess the quality of our clustering. Since this inter-host population is really being generated from some number (k) of subtypes, it follows that entropy models this setting exactly: the lower the entropy, the more likely this is the case. We show that our clustering approach based on CliqueSNV outperforms other standard clustering techniques, such as k-modes, in terms minimizing entropy. Since our clustering achieves such a low entropy, it is an indication that we found the most likely subtypes which represent the data. Because of this, we also employ a procedure to fill gaps in sequences by choosing the closest subtype, rather than using, *e.g.*, a reference sequence. Doing so results in an even lower entropy, indicating that this is a better way to fill gaps.

We validated our approach on the EMBL-EBI dataset. This method very clearly identified the B.1.1.7 subtype corresponding to cluster 6 in Table 5. Since our approach clusters sequences purely on genomic content, we also use a measure of cluster fitness to predict how contagious the identified subtypes may be. Indeed the fitness of this B.1.1.7 subtype (its corresponding cluster) was outstanding, further strengthening this result, and illustrating how this method could be used to detect future variants of concern.

In conclusion, we clearly demonstrate that clustering is a suitable alternative to phylogenetic methods for identifying strains or subtypes. Moreover, since clustering is much faster than constructing phylogenies (which is a computationally intense procedure), our approach is much more scalable to the size of the current datasets. Indeed, by considering the entire dataset all at once, when coupled with fitness, our approach can be a powerful tool for pinpointing a subtype which has the potential to become as pervasive as the B.1.1.7 in the UK, even at the moment when it comprises as little as 1% of the current population.

Acknowledgments. AM, SK, BS, RH and AZ were partially supported from NSF Grant 16119110, and NIH grant 1R01EB025022-01. FM and PS were partially supported from NIH grant 1R01EB025022-01. AM, BS and SK were partially supported by a GSU Molecular Basis of Disease Fellowship. MP was supported by a GSU startup grant.

References

1. EMBL-EBI: Wellcome Genome Campus, Hinxton, Cambridgeshire
2. Ahn, S., Vikalo, H.: aBayesQR: a Bayesian method for reconstruction of viral populations characterized by low diversity. In: Sahinalp, S.C. (ed.) RECOMB 2017. LNCS, vol. 10229, pp. 353–369. Springer, Cham (2017). https://doi.org/10.1007/978-3-319-56970-3_22
3. Anderberg, M.: Cluster Analysis for Applications. Academic Press, Cambridge (1973)
4. Baaijens, J.A., El Aabidine, A.Z., Rivals, E., Schönhuth, A.: De novo assembly of viral quasispecies using overlap graphs. Genome Res. **27**(5), 835–848 (2017)
5. Bukhari, Q., Jameel, Y., Massaro, J., D'Agostino, R., Khan, S.: Periodic oscillations in daily reported infections and deaths for coronavirus disease 2019. JAMA Netw. Open **3**(8), e2017521 (2020). https://doi.org/10.1001/jamanetworkopen.2020.17521
6. Caliński, T., Harabasz, J.: A dendrite method for cluster analysis. Commun. Stat. **3**(1), 1–27 (1974). https://doi.org/10.1080/03610927408827101
7. Ciccolella, S., Patterson, M., Bonizzoni, P., Vedova, G.D.: Effective clustering for single cell sequencing cancer data. In: The 10th ACM International Conference on Bioinformatics, Computational Biology and Health Informatics, ACM-BCB, Niagara Falls, NY, USA, pp. 437–446. ACM (2019). https://doi.org/10.1145/3307339.3342149
8. Ciccolella, S., et al.: Inferring cancer progression from single-cell sequencing while allowing mutation losses. Bioinformatics **37**(3), 326–333 (2020). https://doi.org/10.1093/bioinformatics/btaa722
9. Ciccolella, S., Soto, M., Patterson, M.D., Vedova, G.D., Hajirasouliha, I., Bonizzoni, P.: gpps: an ILP-based approach for inferring cancer progression with mutation losses from single cell data. BMC Bioinform. **21** (2020). Article number: 413. https://doi.org/10.1186/s12859-020-03736-7
10. The COVID-19 Genomics UK (COG-UK) Consortium: An integrated national scale SARS-CoV-2 genomic surveillance network. Lancet Microbe **1**(3), 99–100 (2020)
11. Davies, D.L., Bouldin, D.W.: A cluster separation measure. IEEE Trans. Pattern Anal. Mach. Intell. **PAMI-1**(2), 224–227 (1979). https://doi.org/10.1109/TPAMI.1979.4766909
12. Elbe, S., Buckland-Merrett, G.: Data, disease and diplomacy: GISAID's innovative contribution to global health. Glob. Chall. **1**, 33–46 (2017). https://doi.org/10.1002/gch2.1018
13. Public Health England: Investigation of novel SARS-CoV-2 variant: variant of concern 202012/01. Technical briefing 1 (2021)
14. Hadfield, J., et al.: Nextstrain: real-time tracking of pathogen evolution. Bioinformatics **34**(23), 4121–4123 (2018). https://doi.org/10.1093/bioinformatics/bty407
15. Huang, Z.: A fast clustering algorithm to cluster very large categorical data sets in data mining. In: The SIGMOD Workshop on Research Issues on Data Mining and Knowledge Discovery, pp. 1–8 (1997)
16. Huang, Z.: Extensions to the k-means algorithm for clustering large data sets with categorical values. Data Min. Knowl. Discov. **2**(3), 283–304 (1998). https://doi.org/10.1023/A:1009769707641
17. Jahn, K., Kuipers, J., Beerenwinkel, N.: Tree inference for single-cell data. Genome Biol. **17**(1) (2016). Article number: 86. https://doi.org/10.1186/s13059-016-0936-x
18. James, B., Luczak, B., Girgis, H.: MeShClust: an intelligent tool for clustering DNA sequences. Nucleic Acid Res. **46**(14) (2018). https://doi.org/10.1093/nar/gky315
19. Kammonen, J.I., et al.: gapFinisher: a reliable gap filling pipeline for SSPACE-LongRead scaffolder output (2019). https://doi.org/10.1371/journal.pone.0216885
20. Knyazev, S., Hughes, L., Skums, P., Zelikovsky, A.: Epidemiological data analysis of viral quasispecies in the next-generation sequencing era. Brief. Bioinform. (2020). https://doi.org/10.1093/bib/bbaa101

21. Knyazev, S., et al.: CliqueSNV: scalable reconstruction of intra-host viral populations from NGS reads. bioRxiv (2018). https://doi.org/10.1101/264242

22. Li, T., Ma, S., Ogihara, M.: Entropy-based criterion in categorical clustering. In: Twenty-First International Conference on Machine Learning (2004). https://doi.org/10.1145/1015330.1015404

23. McQueen, J.: Some methods for classification and analysis of multivariate observations. In: The 5th Berkely Symposium on Mathematical Statistics and Probability, pp. 281–297 (1967)

24. du Plessis, L., et al.: Establishment and lineage dynamics of the SARS-CoV-2 epidemic in the UK. Science (2021). https://doi.org/10.1126/science.abf2946

25. Prabhakaran, S., Rey, M., Zagordi, O., Beerenwinkel, N., Roth, V.: HIV haplotype inference using a propagating Dirichlet process mixture model. IEEE/ACM Trans. Comput. Biol. Bioinform. (TCBB) 11(1), 182–191 (2014)

26. Rousseeuw, P.J.: Silhouettes: a graphical aid to the interpretation and validation of cluster analysis. J. Comput. Appl. Math. 20, 53–65 (1987). https://doi.org/10.1016/0377-0427(87)90125-7

27. Schneider, T.D., Stephens, R.: Sequence logos: a new way to display consensus sequences. Nucleic Acids Res. 18(20), 6097–6100 (1990). https://doi.org/10.1093/nar/18.20.6097

28. Skums, P., Campo, D.S., Dimitrova, Z., Vaughan, G., Lau, D.T., Khudyakov, Y.: Numerical detection, measuring and analysis of differential interferon resistance for individual HCV intra-host variants and its influence on the therapy response. Silico Biol. 11(5), 263–269 (2011)

29. Skums, P., Kirpich, A., Baykal, P.I., Zelikovsky, A., Chowell, G.: Global transmission network of SARS-CoV-2: from outbreak to pandemic. medRxiv (2020). https://doi.org/10.1101/2020.03.22.20041145

30. Tamura, K., Nei, M.: Estimation of the number of nucleotide substitutions in the control region of mitochondrial DNA in humans and chimpanzees. Mol. Biol. Evol. 10(3), 512–526 (1993)

31. Tibshirani, R., Walther, G., Hastie, T.: Estimating the number of clusters in a data set via the gap statistic. J. Roy. Stat. Soc. 63(2), 411–423 (2001)

32. Volz, E., et al.: Transmission of SARS-CoV-2 lineage b.1.1.7 in England: insights from linking epidemiological and genetic data. medRxiv (2021). https://doi.org/10.1101/2020.12.30.20249034

33. Vrbik, I., Stephens, D.A., Roger, M., Brenner, B.G.: The Gap Procedure: for the identification of phylogenetic clusters in HIV-1 sequence data. BMC Bioinform. 16(1), 355 (2015). https://doi.org/10.1186/s12859-015-0791-x

34. W.H.O.: update, December 2020

35. Wu, F., et al.: A new coronavirus associated with human respiratory disease in China. Nature 579(7798), 265–269 (2020). https://doi.org/10.1038/s41586-020-2008-3

36. Zhou, P., et al.: A pneumonia outbreak associated with a new coronavirus of probable bat origin. Nature 579(7798), 270–273 (2020). https://doi.org/10.1038/s41586-020-2012-7

Author Index

Printed in the United States
by Baker & Taylor Publisher Services